THE
Quotable
HUBERT H. HUMPHREY

Compiled and Edited
by PERRY D. HALL
and the Staff of *Quote*

DROKE HOUSE, Publishers

ANDERSON, S. C.

Distributed by
GROSSET AND DUNLAP
51 Madison Avenue, New York, N. Y.
G. & D. No. 6700

Library of Congress Catalog Card Number: 67–13267

Published by DROKE HOUSE, Publishers
Anderson, S. C.

MANUFACTURED IN THE UNITED STATES OF AMERICA
DESIGNED BY W. J. MC INTOSH

THE
Quotable
HUBERT H. HUMPHREY

Contents

Introduction

Hubert Humphrey's name has become synonymous with Liberal thought in mid-century America. He has fought hard, and usually victoriously, in battles on the side of Liberal causes, political and social.

As a Professor of Political Science, as Mayor of Minneapolis, then Senator from Minnesota, Senate Whip and, now as Vice President of The United States, he has carried his cause to all sections of the country, to friend and foe alike, and his position has always been clear—and staunch.

Certainly there is no more masterful public speaker on the American political scene today. And the quotations in these pages have been chosen expressly to illustrate—in his own eloquent style—where Hubert H. Humphrey stands on all issues.

It has been an enjoyable challenge, as well as a liberal education, to pore over the manuscripts, speeches, transcripts and articles from which quotes were extracted for this book.

PERRY D. HALL
1967

QUOTATIONS

· · A · ·

ACADEMIC FREEDOM

... Academic freedom is not just an academic matter. It is both the symptom and the cause of other freedoms we enjoy. As John Milton and John Stuart Mill understood in past centuries, the right of free inquiry and of responsible dissent is society's self-correcting mechanism. In a more modern idiom, it is our self-regulating system of "feedback."   [1

Rutgers University
New Brunswick, New Jersey
September 22, 1966

... Even in times of considerable national hysteria, our great universities and colleges have maintained the essential values of free teaching, free discussion and freedom of research.   [2

Georgetown University
Washington, D. C.
March 25, 1966

ACADEMIC RESPONSIBILITY

... I do not believe that our country is passing through a period of academic irresponsibility. Quite the contrary. But I

3

do believe that we cannot, in this age of both danger and promise, demand anything less of ourselves than the most stringent standards. Now, more than ever, the great work of challenging orthodoxies, discovering truths and establishing options is a necessity for human survival and progress.   [3

> *Rutgers University*
> *New Brunswick, New Jersey*
> *September 22, 1966*

ACTION

. . . The people of America want imagination and determination and commitment. They want action. They want performance, not public relations. They want performance, not promises. They want performance, not pleas for patience. [4

> *Americana Hotel*
> *New York, New York*
> *October 31, 1966*

. . . Thomas Huxley once said: "The great end of life is not knowledge, but action." It seems to me an abysmal waste of time, of resources, and of energy whenever men build barriers between themselves or when they miss the opportunity to improve mankind's general lot on earth.   [5

> *Department of Commerce Symposium*
> *on Technology and World Trade*
> *Washington, D. C.*
> *November 16, 1966*

AGRICULTURE

. . . We believe the farmers and the farm families of

America should share in America's prosperity and should not be relegated to last place at the table by a "don't know, don't care" Republican Administration.   [6

Democratic State Convention
Little Rock, Arkansas
September 18, 1964

... Farm people, their problems, their defeats, their triumphs, and their basic importance to our society have been the concern of President Johnson and myself for many years. We come from rural America. We've seen farm depressions, and their terrible human toll, and we never want to see another.   [7

*American Agricultural
Editors' Association
Washington, D. C.
June 22, 1966*

... The American farmer with his abundance is making a lasting contribution to our health, to our national prosperity, and to peace in the world. The farmer has become the soldier of peace for this nation. And the farmer with his system of distribution has been a bulwark of strength for our country. He is entitled to, and should receive, his fair share of our prosperity.   [8

*American Agricultural
Editors' Association
Washington, D. C.
June 22, 1966*

... We Americans are good competitors. The American farmer is the best. He stands as the all-time undefeated, champion, unchallenged, unexcelled producingest person on earth.   [9

Nebraska Corn-Picking Contest
Utica, Nebraska
October 4, 1966

AMERICA

... We are the standard-bearers in the only really authentic revolution, the democratic revolution against tyrannies. Our strength is not to be measured by our military capacity alone, by our industry, or by our technology. We will be remembered, not for the power of our weapons, but for the power of our compassion, our dedication to human welfare.

That welfare demands that full scope be given to social as well as mechanical invention. The founders of this nation understood this and sought to secure conditions favorable to the pursuit of happiness. They recognized man's spiritual nature, and the needs of emotion and intellect. They knew that only part of the pain and pleasure of life is to be found in material things.

Each person has capacities not possessed by any other. The free society alone can release these capacities. The fact is that we have released human creative talent to a greater degree than ever before in history. The productive power of American industry is one proof of this. But we need to extend this creative power into the cultural and spiritual areas of life. And we need to prove that human brotherhood, under freedom, has more power to fire the imagination of peoples of the world than any purely materialistic system. Viewed in these terms, brotherhood has never before been so strong a requirement for our national security.

I see, in the America of tomorrow, the true spiritual and cultural capital of the world. It will be heir to man's loftiest hopes and achievements. It will be a land of many races and religions, of peoples cosmopolitan and understanding of each other—yet each cherishing their unique traditions. It will be a land such as never existed before, and it will vibrate with the creativity and unleashed talents of millions.   [10

"The Cause Is Mankind"
(Praeger)

... Our founding fathers did not establish this republic merely to ensure its citizens of life, liberty, and security. They aimed much, much higher—they declared the rights to "life, liberty, and the pursuit of happiness." Even a totalitarian state can offer total security. But only an open society can offer its citizens the freedom to seek self-fulfillment in their own way—and that, I think, is the real meaning of happiness.   [11

University of Chicago
Chicago, Illinois
January 14, 1966

... If we can build in America a society operating on all its cylinders, others in the world may have some hope of doing the same. If we cannot, what hope may others have?
          [12

Associated Press
New York, New York
April 25, 1966

7

... During the past several weeks, I've been traveling across America. And, as I've been going places, the most vivid impression I get is of an America that's going places. We've almost taken progress for granted. In America today progress and innovation are the status quo. If you're just moving, you're falling backward. If you're standing still, you're nowhere.   [13

Town Hall Rally
Philadelphia, Pennsylvania
October 4, 1966

... It is the special blessing of this land, that each generation of Americans has called its own cadence, and written its own music—and our greatest songs are still unsung.   [14

Michigan State University
East Lansing, Michigan
June 12, 1966

... Let us strive to build an America of new faith in old dreams—an America eternally vigorous and creative. Let us preserve America as a reservoir of hope and faith in the midst of cynicism and despair.   [15

National Student Association
University of Wisconsin
August 23, 1965

... We need an America with the wisdom of experience. But we must not let America grow old in spirit.   [16

Speech
1965

8

... The deepest concern of America is not only for its poor but for all its people; not only for the economic problems of the moment, but for life in all its dimensions and the possibilities of a richer life in the future. For the problems of the future as seen and known *now*, are our problems.   [17

"War on Poverty"
McGraw-Hill

... **Strength.** The real strength of America is not in government. It is in America's businessmen, its workers, its farmers, its professional people. It is in its wide array of non-governmental organizations—its churches, its civic groups, its trade associations and trade unions, its professional societies, its universities, and—not least—its political parties.   [18

University of Chicago
January 14, 1966

AMERICA (IMAGE OF)

... Let the word go forth that America is a life-giving nation, not a life-taking nation.   [19

Huron College
Huron, South Dakota
May 31, 1966

... We have a fixation on being able to portray the riots, the violence, the disease, the destruction, the despair that

9

afflicts us. There ought to be some balance, and I appeal to you for that balance.   [20

American Agricultural
Editors' Association
Washington, D. C.
June 22, 1966

... We must begin by facing a painful fact. In much of the world, the image of the United States is that of the guardian of the status quo. It is that of the harried mother who tells her maid: "Go find out what the children are doing, and tell them to stop it." This would be a cause for real regret even if the status quo were reliably durable or widely popular. But it is neither.   [21

Foreign Service Association
Washington, D. C.
May 26, 1966

AMERICANS

... There is in every American, I think, something of the old Daniel Boone—who, when he could see the smoke from another chimney, felt himself too crowded and moved further out into the wilderness.   [22

University of Chicago
January 14, 1966

... In many ways, we Americans are today a conservative people—for the very good reason that we have so much that is worthwhile to conserve. It is not easy for us to realize that most other peoples have not been similarly blessed by history.   [23

> *Foreign Service Association*
> *Washington, D. C.*
> *May 26, 1966*

ARMS RACE

... Every day the costly and dangerous arms race proceeds man not only increases his risk of annihilation, but decreases his possibilities for a more satisfying life on earth.   [24

> *Weizmann Institute Dinner*
> *New York City*
> *December 6, 1965*

... There is no long run security in a great arms race—only an increasingly volatile insecurity in which one mistake or miscalculation can trigger Armageddon. Each new weapon breeds a counterweapon. An arms race saps the resources of rich and poor alike. It sets in motion forces of power politics and mutual fear. It poisons the well-springs of international cooperation.   [25

> *Buffalo Club*
> *Buffalo, New York*
> *January 6, 1967*

THE ARTS

... I think that the good life, the civilized life, is more

11

than bread, more than automobiles, more than refrigerators—it is poetry, it is drama, it is music and all the arts. [26

North Carolina Mutual Life Insurance
Company Building Dedication
Durham, North Carolina
April 2, 1966

ASIA

... The inescapable agony and pain of Vietnam have compelled us to face the stark realities of an Asia in turmoil and revolution. Nowhere are the challenges more formidable than they are in Asia, where two-thirds of the human race lives. Asia is rich in peoples, rich in culture and rich in resources. It is also rich in trouble.   [27

National Convention
Americans for Democratic Action
Washington, D. C.
April 23, 1966

... We will have to learn far more about Asian history and Asian cultures than any of us now know. We need more than nodding acquaintance with the key critical issues that absorb the attention of Asians. We will have to learn to speak and read the Asian languages. We will have to become more sensitive to the differences among Asian nations as well as their similarities.   [28

West Point, New York
June 8, 1966

... Asia means people—more than half of mankind. Asia means civilizations—venerable, inventive, artistic, and deeply rooted cultures. Asia means religions—the great compassionate religious and ethical systems of Hinduism, Confucianism, Buddhism, Islam and Christianity. Asia means problems—the age-old afflictions of poverty, illiteracy, disease, exploitation, and oppression. And in the modern era—the past hundred years or so—Asia means revolution.

[29

West Point, New York
June 8, 1966

...We shall persevere and explore means of communication and exchange, looking to the day when the leaders of Asian communism—as their former colleagues in Europe—will come to recognize the self-destructiveness and wastefulness of their present bellicose policies.   [30

West Point, New York
June 8, 1966

ATLANTIC COMMUNITY

...The Atlantic nations cannot survive as an island of stability in a world of chaos.   [31

NATO Parliamentarians
New York City
October 5, 1965

...Our true self-interest is served by a view of international affairs which emphasizes mutual assistance as well as competitive coexistence. If I am unrealistic, so were the men who had the audacity to dream of a united, peaceful Europe at the close of mankind's most dreadful war. If I am unrealistic, so are other men today who see the possibilities of a world without fences . . . a world in which all nations live together in common harmony and in peace rather than in rivalry and war.

I happen to believe that to be realistic today is to reach for these things. I believe it is highly unrealistic to think that mankind can follow any other course with any other result than antagonism, peril and the possibility, finally, of nuclear destruction.

Twenty years ago, we in America made basic decisions about the direction of our international policy. We did not turn inward upon ourselves nor did we return to the dangerous isolationist policies of the past. We committed ourselves to our partners—to their survival and well-being.

Now we are at another time of decision. There are voices raised in our country and in other countries which call again for a return to the old inwardness. But I believe that we shall overcome them, just as I believe the people of the nations of Europe will overcome the same voices within their borders. As man's life changes, so must man's institutions. And today we and our partners must shape our common institutions so that they may be able to meet tomorrow's priorities and not yesterday's. For the essence of statesmanship is not a rigid adherence to the past, but a prudent and probing concern for the future. We must preserve what is good. We must add that which strengthens.   [32

US Chiefs of Mission Conference
Bonn, Germany
March 30, 1967

ATOMIC AGE

... Ours is a new era, one which calls for a new kind of courage. For the first time in the history of mankind, one generation literally has the power to destroy the past, the present and the future, the power to bring time to an end.

[33

New York City
October 29, 1964

... Prudence and reason, not the slogans of the past, will guide us as we try to reduce the unacceptable risks of ignorance and misunderstanding in a thermonuclear age.   [34

West Point, New York
June 8, 1966

... In this world, disaster is ever but a step away. There is no margin for error.   [35

Acceptance Address
Democratic Convention
August 28, 1964

... Statesmen—who bear a heavier responsibility than others—cannot ignore the implications for the survival of mankind of new discoveries in technology, biology, nuclear physics and space. In this nuclear age the deliberate initiation of full-scale war as an instrument of national policy has become folly. Originally a means to protect national interests, war today can assure the death of a nation, the decima-

15

tion of a continent. Nuclear power has placed into the hands of men the power to destroy all that man has created. Only responsible statesmen—who perceive that perseverance in the pursuit of peace is not cowardice, but courage, that restraint in the use of force is not weakness, but wisdom—can prevent present international rivalries from leading to an incinerated world. [36

Pacem in Terris Conference
New York City
February 17, 1965

·· B ··

BALANCE

... Clearly one of the main streams of Western thought—cradled in the life of the great Western colleges and universities—has been the principle of balance, of equilibrium, of symmetry. [37

*National Conference on
Higher Education*
1959

BIRTH

... I was born over a drug store. They were short of log cabins that year. [38

BROTHERHOOD

... I feel within me the certainty that all the men in the world *are* brothers, irrespective of the imaginary boundaries we may draw between ourselves. [39

*Memorial Service for
Prime Minister Shastri
Washington Cathedral
January 28, 1966*

17

... America is so blessed. And I am proud when America steps forward and says to the less fortunate of the world: "We *are* our brother's keeper."   [40

Al Smith Dinner
New York City
October 13, 1965

... We are often denounced for our materialism, but I believe that no society in the world is more willing than America to fulfill the obligations of human brotherhood, to aid the sick, feed the hungry.   [41

New York City
October 29, 1964

BUDGET POLICY

... An aggressive approach to economy in government does more than merely show where budget cuts can be made. It provides a sound systematic basis for intelligent and responsible planning. A budget thus becomes not merely a column of figures, but a series of choices, and with each choice the alternative is clearly stated.   [42

Business Council
Hot Springs, Virginia
October 15, 1965

BUSINESS

... There are almost five million American business firms with paid employees. Counting farms, we have about nine million sole proprietors and over two million partners. Such figures demonstrate how radically mistaken is the Communist concept of an economy marching to the tune of a handful of capitalists.   [43

"Big Business: Is It Too Big?"
Look Magazine
May 22, 1962

... American business. American business is more progressive than any politician and in a sense more revolutionary and radical than any American political party. It is this American business system of ours that has developed consumer credit, health and welfare programs for its employees, supported our colleges and universities, and accumulated the wealth and resources for a vast system of philanthropy and charity. I am proud of such a system. I don't care how you describe it—'liberal' or 'conservative.' I like it and will do my best to protect it, defend it, and encourage it. [44

Interview
October 1965

... American business is doing a splendid job. But somebody ought to say once in a while how well it is done—by avoiding excesses of inventories, by keeping down unnecessary costs, by offering more and better goods and services to customers. And may I say this so it can be heard outside America: no single business group in the world is so humane, as progressive, as liberal as the American businessman and the American business community.   [45

Industrial Press Service
1966

... **Individuality.** It is the businessman who, of all citizens, most clearly knows what many others but dimly see: That much of our American progress has been the product of the individual who had an idea; pursued it; fashioned it; tenaciously clung to it against all odds; and then produced it, sold it, and profited from it.   [46

> *United States Junior*
> *Chamber of Commerce*
> *Detroit, Michigan*
> *June 29, 1966*

... **Youth.** Young Americans must know that individuality and initiative *are* a part of the daily environment of business, that new ideas are greeted with enthusiasm, and that business is not just profit and loss, but also the business of the community and of responsible citizenship.   [47

> *United States Junior*
> *Chamber of Commerce*
> *Detroit, Michigan*
> *June 29, 1966*

BUSINESS AND GOVERNMENT

... I believe in the profit system—and I also believe that it can work even more effectively than it has in the past for the public good. For too long, business and government entrenched themselves on opposite sides of an imaginary line—the line dividing the so-called "private sector" from the so-called "public sector"—and glowered at one another. Some businessmen suspected government of an insatiable appetite to expand its functions, and to encroach upon private enterprise, and ultimately to stifle it. Some government officials regarded business as inherently oblivious or even antagonistic to the public interest. Some even regarded profits as actually immoral—rather than as an incentive essential to efficiency, as even the Communists are now coming to recognize. These old suspicions are fading rapidly into history, and mutual confidence and cooperation are replacing them. I for one am glad of it. I do not believe that government has any monopoly of wisdom—or of dedication to the public good. I think we need to draw upon the ability, the energy, and the innovating talents of *all* elements of the community in dealing with the problems which confront us.

[48

International Newspaper
Advertising Executives
Washington, D. C.
January 26, 1967

BUSINESS AND PUBLIC NEEDS

... The past few years, in our country, have been years of amazing technological and material progress and innovation. There has been a need for these things, and it has been met.

But we also need social inventiveness, and social innovation, and we need to create a market for them as well.

We have urgent and keenly-felt public needs, most of them coming to a focus in the great urban areas where two-thirds of us already live and an even higher proportion will live in the future.

But there has been no place, by and large, where people could go to shop for a better public school system . . . for the means of eliminating poverty and racial discrimination . . . for unsnarling our traffic jams, or for ridding our air and water of their perilous pollution.

I go further, I believe that we should seek to make meeting public needs actually *profitable* for private enterprise. We ought to create markets in meeting these needs, for which companies can compete just as they do in designing and selling automobiles or television sets.

Therefore, I am delighted that, in our war on poverty, we have given corporations the opportunity to operate Job Corps Camps at a profit—and, indeed, to compete in seeing who can set up and run the best one. For I am convinced that, once business has had a real taste of helping the poor—and doing it profitably—we will have come a long way in fully unharnessing the energy and ingenuity that lies within our country.

Profit *and* morality are a hard combination to beat.   [49

International Newspaper
Advertising Executives
Washington, D. C.
January 26, 1967

· · C · ·

CENSORSHIP

... None of us would trade freedom of expression and of
ideas for the narrowness of the public censor. America is a
free market for people who have something to say, and need
not fear to say it. It is your job, and it is mine, to see that
America remains that way.   [50

> *National Book Awards*
> *New York City*
> *March 8, 1967*

CHANGE (NEED OF)

... One test of democratic government is its ability to
respond rapidly to changing conditions.   [51

> *"Making Cities Fit For People"*
> Saturday Review
> *July 3, 1965*

... Hubert Humphrey is no "status quo" man. He is for
change—change to meet the needs and priorities of the
times.   [52

> *National Governors Conference*
> *Los Angeles, California*
> *July 6, 1966*

... If there is dissatisfaction with the status quo, good. If there is ferment, so much the better. If there is restlessness, I am pleased. Then let there be ideas, and hard thought, and hard work. If man feels small, let man make himself bigger. Ours is that opportunity. Let us make the most of it.   [53

University of Chicago
January 14, 1966

... **Values.**   In your search for identity and self-knowledge, you will have much to discover before you determine what is worthwhile, and what is worthless. But in a land of individuals, better the mystery of the search than some counterfeit security. In a world society desperate for change, better your dedication to it than your fear of it.   [54

Michigan State University
East Lansing, Michigan
June 12, 1966

CHILDREN

... Each child is an adventure into a better life—an opportunity to change the old pattern and make it new.   [55

League of Cities
Detroit, Michigan
July 27, 1965

CHINA

... Today we see in mainland China the tragic result of

an Asian revolution that lost its way—a revolution captured by a disciplined Communist minority.   [56

West Point, New York
June 8, 1966

... We seek and will continue to seek to build bridges, to keep open the doors of communication, to the Communist states of Asia, and in particular Communist China. The isolation of the Asian Communist states—however caused—breeds unreality, delusion, and miscalculation. [57

West Point, New York
June 8, 1966

... **Friendship.** I am convinced that—despite the shrill anti-American propaganda which is carried on by the Chinese Communists—there is still much friendship for us among the Chinese people, from our many previous years of fruitful and constructive work together.   [58

*Columbia Scholastic
Press Association
New York City
March 12, 1966*

CHURCHES

... Some local churches still erect racial barriers at their doors—and many more do not speak out affirmatively on urgent questions of racial justice which arise in our communities.   [59

*White House Conference
"To Fulfill These Rights"
June 1, 1966*

. . . The entry of American churches and synagogues not only into the struggle for human rights—but for economic and social justice as well—has made a tremendous difference in our country. I cannot think where we would be today without this massive injection of activated faith.   [60

National Conference of
Christians and Jews
New York City
June 28, 1966

CHURCHMEN

. . . A great and growing number of religious leaders and laymen have given stirring witness that their faith is anything but lifeless. They joined in the March on Washington three years ago. They marched, less comfortably and far more dangerously, from Selma to Montgomery and through Mississippi. They have been at work in remote and downtrodden areas of the South. They have braved the degradation and potential violence of our Northern slums. They are the stuff of which saints and martyrs are made. They have borne the heat of the day and the perils of the night. They have given their all—and in some cases their lives—for the real brotherhood of man under the Fatherhood of God.   [61

National Conference of
Christians and Jews
New York City
June 28, 1966

. . . **Evildoers.** Through history, magistrates and theologians have had a mutual interest in the sin and evil of the

26

world. As Mayor of Minneapolis I spent much of my time "restraining evil doers"—to use Martin Luther's terms—a function which, on occasion, also falls to religion.   [62

> *National Conference of*
> *Christians and Jews*
> *New York City*
> *June 28, 1966*

...**Involvement.** One of the most heartening developments in recent history has been the growing realization among men of all religions that the tenets of their faiths necessarily lead them to confront—and to combat—human suffering, misery and injustice wherever they are found. [63

> *Convention of National Catholic*
> *Social Action Conference*
> *Georgetown University*
> *Washington, D. C.*
> *August 26, 1966*

...**Politicians.** Churchmen are accustomed to taking a longer view than politicians. We political leaders often feel we are doing well if we can see to the end of next year—or to the end of our term of office. But you churchmen look at events in the aspect of eternity.   [64

> *National Council of Churches*
> *Miami, Florida*
> *December 7, 1966*

CITIES

... In the Middle Ages, sober and civilized citizens surrounded their cities with high, fortified walls. The gates in these walled cities were closed at night to keep out the savage marauders of the countryside. Today, in the middle of the twentieth century, we are in danger of creating new walled cities—but cities from which the "sober and civilized citizens" will largely have fled—cities in which violence lies on the *inside*, cities in which the remaining inhabitants will be surrounded not by walls of stone, but by unbreachable social, economic and political barriers.   [65

Urban America Conference
Washington, D. C.
September 13, 1966

. . . We are in danger—in a society that prides itself on being an open society, in a society that espouses the democratic ideal—of making our central cities not centers of enlightenment and higher aspiration, but stagnant and congested places to be avoided except on the most necessary missions of commerce or of politics. We are in danger—unless we act wisely and quickly—of making our cities places where business goes on but where life, in its real sense, is lost.   [66

Urban America Conference
Washington, D. C.
September 13, 1966

. . . I would only say this: just men, just money, just material—no matter how high the level of each—will not be enough to make our American cities what we want them to

28

be. The way lies open to cities filled with green and open space, to transportation that is safe, comfortable, rapid, to neighborhoods once more filled with neighbors, to schools and universities that truly care about the future of our children, to rural areas, towns, cities, suburbs where people, because they are citizens, because they are people, can live together in harmony and cooperation, no matter what their age, the color of their skin, their religion, or their last name.

[67

Urban America Conference
Washington, D. C.
September 13, 1966

... We are challenged to make our cities decent places in which to live and learn, to work and play. A vast sprawling motorized population—living impersonally with computerized institutions—must somehow again become a community. [68

Southern Conference on Education
Richmond, Virginia
December 2, 1965

... **Small.** Small cities as well as large ones face the converging forces of growth and decay. They are also plagued with slums, urban blight, traffic and parking problems, cascading demands for services and the shortage of tax revenues to meet them. [69

Regional Conference of Mayors
Cleveland, Ohio
May 6, 1966

... Solutions. Government, business, labor, and our universities should combine and coordinate their resources and their creative capacities to meet the great over-riding need of making our cities fit places in which to live.   [70

> *International Newspaper*
> *Advertising Executives*
> *Washington, D. C.*
> *January 26, 1967*

CIVIL RIGHTS

... There are those who say to you—we are rushing this issue of civil rights. I say we are 172 years late. There are those who say—this issue of civil rights is an infringement on states rights. The time has arrived for the Democratic party to get out of the shadow of state's rights and walk forthrightly into the bright sunshine of human rights.   [71

> *As Mayor of Minneapolis*
> *Addressing the Democratic National Conv.*
> *Philadelphia, July 14, 1948*
> *Supporting his Civil Rights Amendment*
>   *to the Party Platform*

... We can rejoice that the time has arrived when millions of Negro Americans can step out of the shadows, and walk forthrightly into the bright sunshine of human rights. But a man too long walled off from his fellows cannot easily adjust his senses and his capacities to the light—and the heat—of equality. This generation of Americans has the task, and the priceless opportunity, of walking side by side with the Negro American as he strides into that bright sunshine and stands erect. [72

White House Conference
"To Fulfill These Rights"
June 1, 1966

... In a few short years, we have traveled down a road studded with landmarks: historic Supreme Court decisions, legislative victories, executive actions. And as we have traveled that road, we have seen thousands of acts of heroism, large and small, by the brave and determined Americans who made that journey with us—men and women of both races struggling to secure the reality of freedom, equality and human dignity. [73

White House Conference
"To Fulfill These Rights"
June 1, 1966

... Twenty million Americans will no longer be pacified by slogans or tokens. They will not be satisfied—they shall not be moved—nor should they be. For "Freedom Now" is not a catchword for a minority of Americans. It is a moral imperative for all Americans. [74

White House Conference
"To Fulfill These Rights"
June 1, 1966

... We should have learned by now that laws and court decisions can only point the way. They can establish criteria of right and wrong. And they can provide a basis for rooting out the evils of bigotry and racism. But they cannot wipe away centuries of oppression and injustice—however much we might desire it.   [75

White House Conference
"To Fulfill These Rights"
June 1, 1966

. . . We cannot avoid the realization that many times our deeds have not matched our words—that there still exists a tragic gap separating promise from performance in many crucial areas of civil rights policy. The blame for that gap cannot be laid at the feet of any single person, or institution. Every major segment of society has contributed to maintaining this gap between promise and performance.   [76

White House Conference
"To Fulfill these Rights"
June 1, 1966

. . . I urge you, as I urge all Americans, to view the civil rights movement not in the harsh glare, the distorted reflection of today's headlines, but rather in the more balanced perspective of history . . . Do not allow your convictions to be uprooted, your steadfast course altered by the occasional excesses, the temporary aberrations which, history tells us, must be experiences in any great movement toward social justice.   [77

White House Conference
"To Fulfill These Rights"
June 1, 1966

... We marched, (and I underscored the word "we") and fought for the end to lynching. We marched and fought against separate and unequal education, and segregated lunch counters, and for a seat in the front of the bus rather than the back of the bus. There have been defeats. But, my fellow Americans, there have been many more victories. [78

NAACP National Convention
Los Angeles, California
July 6, 1966

... There are no instant solutions to problems generations in the making. But there are certain problems demanding priority, yes, immediate attention as we strive to translate legal promises of equality and freedom into reality.   [79

NAACP Convention
Los Angeles, California
July 6, 1966

... The Negro American asks: Are my children attending better schools? Do I hold a better job or any job? Do I have a voice in the life of my city, in my neighborhood? Am I a first class citizen, a man among men in my own eyes and in the eyes of my family? These are the questions that are being asked. And until a man can truthfully answer "yes" to these questions, we should not expect him to consider the battle won or the struggle ended. And neither should we. For what is left for such a man when the dust of the march is settled? Where today the slogans of a better world spring from his

lips, tomorrow there may be nothing but the taste of ashes.
[80

NAACP Convention
Los Angeles, California
July 6, 1966

. . . We must strive to perfect *one* citizenship, *one* destiny for all Americans. That's our goal. Integration must be recognized as an essential means to *ends* that we are seeking—the ends of freedom and justice and equal opportunity for all Americans.   [81

NAACP National Convention
Los Angeles, California
July 6, 1966

. . . Facts and statistics cannot convey the sense of anxiety and terror which grips the heart of a brave 9 year old Negro girl attending for the first time a newly integrated school—or the hopelessness of an unemployed Negro father who realizes his family will receive more money on welfare than he can provide with his limited skills.   [82

Howard University
Washington, D. C.
September 19, 1966

. . . Facts and statistics, taken alone, can never, never indicate the relief that sweeps over a Negro husband and wife as their sick child is taken to the newly integrated community hospital where first-class medicine is practiced—or the joy and hope that is born anew as a Negro family leaves a rat-infested tenement for a fairly-priced, clean apartment in a safe and attractive neighborhood. [83

Howard University
Washington, D. C.
September 19, 1966

... The wrongs and evils of generations cannot be corrected easily or without sacrifice—just as a mighty storm cannot pass without creating turbulence and unrest. But after that storm comes the brilliant sunshine of a new day—and with the sunshine comes renewed faith and strength. [84

Howard University
Washington, D. C.
September 19, 1966

... **Housing.** People of all races and backgrounds must have the opportunity to purchase or rent housing. Without having to brave insult, indignity and even violence. [85

National Fellowship Awards Dinner
Philadelphia, Pennsylvania
May 23, 1966

... There is a tendency—to which we Americans are prone—to think that it is sufficient to put laws in the statute books. It is not. Laws must be enforced. But even more, they must be observed. That means changing people's minds, opening them up to the wrongs, which, consciously or unconsciously, they have done their fellow Americans. The synagogues and the churches have worked nobly to this purpose, and I appeal to them to redouble their efforts. This is a responsibility for every individual American, as well. In the prophetic tradition, each of us must be able to look to himself and say, in the words of the Prophet Nathan: "Thou art the man!" [86

Adas Israel Synagogue
Washington, D. C.
December 10, 1966

COLLEGES

. . . While colleges have a legitimate role as "islands of contemplation," there is a concurrent responsibility to develop more experienced and toughened young minds than are now being shaped in sheltered academic situations. The campus must open its gates wider to the currents of American and world political, economic, and social opinion. I should like to see the swirl and beat of controversy developing much more freely. I am dismayed when I hear a college official tell an audience that "we won't get into controversial subjects here." Disagreement and dissent are basic to democracy. Where but on a college campus can they be expressed more thoughtfully and to better purpose? Are they not part of the educational process? There is nothing more stimulating to young men and women coming to intellectual maturity than exposure to the realities of politics and public issues

36

of all kinds—and exposure to unpopular, nonconformist, but challenging points of view.   [87

"Cause is Mankind"
Praeger

... I think that the educational institution must move back into the community. It must abandon some of its aspirations for isolation. It must be not a tower of ivory, but a tower of strength in the daily life of the people. We must go back to the early European ideas of the university as part of the city, and away from the English idea—so prevalent here in the 1800's—that the institution of higher learning must be isolated from life by acres and acres of well-tended lawn. You have a great deal to give to your cities, and your cities have a geat deal to give you. There are many community problems which would benefit more from research than from argument, and the university should be in the midst of all of them.   [88

QUOTE Magazine
June, 1967

COMMUNICATIONS

... The Communications explosion has vastly enlarged the role of public diplomacy. May it always be an instrument, in our country, for truth. May it always be an instrument used for man's betterment and emancipation.   [89

Edward R. Murrow Center
of Public Diplomacy
Medford, Massachusetts
December 6, 1965

... One simple invention—the transistor radio—may have had more psychological impact on the world than any other single invention in the past century. For the transistor radio has suddenly become an immensely significant political instrument. People everywhere today are now within earshot of a transistor radio. Most of these people today are in the new nations that have erupted into the political scene since the end of World War II. Their village views are backed up by their village votes. These people in the remote villages of the world may not be literate in the traditional sense. But they *are* politically conscious. They are in touch. They know what is going on. And they will help shape the future of mankind.   [90

Edward R. Murrow Center
of Public Diplomacy
Medford, Massachusetts
December 6, 1965

COMMUNISM VS FREEDOM

... If you believe—as I do—that freedom has a fierce vitality, you will have no fear of the long run consequences of peaceful competition between democracy and communism.   [91

New York City
October 29, 1964

... Underneath the surface of Communist totalitarianism, the force of freedom is seething, the commitment to freedom is spreading. And freedom is the most contagious virus known to man. [92

New York City
October 29, 1964

... This generation of Americans has learned it is not enough to meet the threat of communism abroad with military force alone. We have learned to employ a variety of tools—economic, political, diplomatic and military. [93

Conference with City Managers
Washington, D. C.
July 28, 1966

... **Battle for Men's Minds.** The Communists have been getting away with ideological piracy. They have been quicker than some of our own leaders to recognize the real battleground of the world—the struggle for men's minds—and swifter to understand the surging drives that are toppling kings and emperors and colonialist powers throughout Asia and Africa. [94

National Conference
on Higher Education
1959

... **Elections.** I challenge any Communist regime to hold a national election under our ground rules—with full freedom for campaigning and full access to the proceedings by the world press. If such an election were genuinely free, and if the Communists should by any chance win it, it would be the first time they ever won a free national election anytime, anywhere in the world. It's no wonder that they don't risk free elections. [95

National Convention
Americans for Democratic Action
Washington, D. C.
April 23, 1966

COMPROMISE

... If I believe in something I will fight for it with all I have. But I do not demand all or nothing. I would rather get something than nothing. Professional liberals want the fiery debate. They glory in defeat. The hardest job for a politician today is to have the courage to be moderate. It's easy to take an extreme position. [96

Interview
1965

CONGRESS

... Congress is not a battlefield for blind armies that clash by night; it is a public forum operating in the light of day for men of reason. It is a place where national objectives are sought, were presidential programs are reviewed, where great societies are endlessly debated and implemented. [97

Syracuse University
June 6, 1965

... I have found Congressional service to be a remarkable form of higher education. It's a super-graduate school in every discipline. My teachers have been presidents and department heads, constituents, press, radio, and television, and above all a group of wise and distinguished colleagues in both houses.   [98

Syracuse University
June 6, 1965

... What sometimes seem to the naive and untutored eye to be legislative obstructionisms, often are no more than the honest expressions of dedicated representatives trying to make clear the attitudes and the interests of their states and regions, sometimes trying to gain time for public understanding of vital issues. But ultimately the Congress will behave as the nation behaves, the Congress will represent the spirit of the American people.   [99

Syracuse University
June 6, 1965

... As long as the Congress of the United States continues to function as a responsible and viable element in our Constitutional system, the promise of American democracy will forever endure—the torch of freedom will forever light the path of our future.   [100

Syracuse University
June 6, 1965

... I have seen in the Halls of Congress more idealism, more humaneness, more compassion, more profiles of courage than in any other institution that I have ever known.

[101

Syracuse University
June 6, 1965

... In Congress, we can only vote two ways: aye or nay. If they could vote "maybe" it would be much easier. But you can't vote "maybe."

[102

Economic Club of Detroit
October 22, 1965

CONSERVATION

... We have been blessed with so rich an endowment that we sometimes have been deluded into seeing it as limitless. We took our forests for granted until they were threatened with exhaustion. We misused our high central plains until they began blowing away as dust in the wind. In both these cases, we did wake up and take remedial action—but, as in the old-time movie serials, it was just in the nick of time.

[103

Gannon College
Erie, Pennsylvania
October 11, 1966

42

$\cdot\cdot D \cdot\cdot$

DECISIONS

... Every decision that this nation has had to make in recent years has been one that carried with it terrible risks. When we faced up to the Russians in Berlin, there was always the risk that it might explode into a terrible war. When we faced up to the Russians in Iran immediately after World War II and asked them to get their forces out, there was a risk. When we aided the Greeks in the Greek Civil War, there was the risk of confrontation, once again, with the Soviet Union. And surely in the Cuban missile crisis we were close to terribly destructive war. The Communist leaders must believe that we mean what we say. I think the worst thing this nation could do for humanity would be to leave any uncertainty as to our will, our purpose and our capacity to carry out our purpose. [104

Meet the Press
March 13, 1965

... This administration and any administration that is entrusted with the security of this nation cannot let the political eye govern the decisions that must be made in reference to our national interest and our national security. One of the prices that you pay in public office as an elected official is the risk of making decisions at times that are rather unpopular. [105

Meet The Press
March 13, 1966

... Choice is a vital part of all our lives, and nowhere is it more important than in government; indeed, a wise Frenchman has observed that "to govern is to choose." Each choice taken—indeed, even each choice deferred or avoided—has consequences reaching far into the future. [106

American Council of
Learned Societies
January 20, 1966

DEMOCRACY

... There are three words—"people, progress and peace"—that belong to the lexicon of democracy, and that uniquely represent the democratic tradition. They are powerful words—so important and so powerful that the enemies of freedom have attempted to take them to their bosoms—literally to steal them away. [107

National Conference on
Higher Education
1959

... The glory of the democracy and of the democratic faith is the courage of it, the experimentation of it, and the

44

willingness to try to begin anew, if we should fail, to rise once again, if we should falter, to try once again.   [108

Syracuse University
June 6, 1965

... It is not enough to merely defend democracy. To defend it may be to lose it; to extend it is to strengthen it. Democracy is not property; it is an idea.   [109

Address as State Chief of War Service Section
Minnesota Works Project Administration
At the Annual Conference
  of the Minnesota Library Association
October 1, 1942

... Democracy is a constant challenge; it requires the best of everyone. It cannot be bought in the marketplace; it cannot be merely legislated; its cost is measured in terms of blood, sweat and tears. It is a challenge for the future; it is not a status quo; it requires men of courage and men of boldness; it must be ever restless and desirous of new victories. It is amazingly strong. It lives only where men are willing to think and study, plan and achieve, sacrifice and give. Yes, it is a rocky road, but its durability, its essential perfectability are unequalled.   [110

Address as State Chief of War Services Section
Minnesota Work Projects Administration
At the Annual Conference
  of the Minnesota Library Association
October 1, 1942

45

. . . Democracy takes into account the full range of human nature. It is the only form of government that can guarantee *both* justice and freedom because it is the *only* one that seeks to recognize and respect the legitimate claims of all conflicting interests.   [111

"Christianity and Crisis,"
25th Anniversary
New York City
February 25, 1965

. . . We must always remember that democracy is a human means for achieving human ends. It will grow and flourish only as it produces visible and tangible results for the people—the opportunity for a fuller and better life, freely chosen and freely determined.   [112

Americans for Democratic Action
Washington, D. C.
April 23, 1966

DEMOCRATIC PARTY

. . . We Democrats do plead guilty to being uplifters. And we plead no defense when it comes to talking. But we also know the value of ideas and action. We are not, as Judge Learned Hand once said of our opposition, "Old Tories . . . intellectually moribund . . . emitting dreary sounds." When Democrats meet there may be sound, but there is also motion—motion on behalf of the people.   [113

Democratic Campaign Conference
Washington, D. C.
July 27, 1966

. . . Our opposition will never understand the Democratic Party. Our Party is—to the unpracticed eyes of the old Republican Tories—a mysterious contraption that usually seems to be moving in a thousand directions. What they don't know is what hurts them. For all that movement in the Democratic Party is caused by the internal combustion of creative ferment, of ideas, of people vigorously committed to the proposition that change and social progress are not only to be desired; they are necessities of twentieth century America. [114

Democratic State Convention
Buffalo, New York
September 8, 1966

. . . Whenever I come to a Democratic conference such as this one, I always think of the words of a crusty old farm leader who was in Washington during the early days of the New Deal. His name was George Peek. George Peek said: "The common characteristic of all uplifters is an unquenchable thirst for conversation. They are all chain talkers." [115

Democratic Campaign Conference
Washington, D. C.
July 27, 1966

DISCRIMINATION

. . . All regions and all states have shared in the precious heritage of American freedom. All states and all regions have at least some infringements of that freedom—all people, all groups have been the victims of discrimination. [116

1948 Speech on Civil Rights

... Even if discrimination cost this nation not one penny, we would have the moral obligation to eradicate it. But we must not close our eyes to the staggering costs we incur each year for our failure to open wide the doors of opportunity for every American.   [117

*North Carolina Mutual Life
Insurance Company Building Dedication
Durham, North Carolina
April 2, 1966*

... It seems to me fundamental that we cannot embrace the dogma of the oppressors—that notion that somehow a person's skin color determines his worthiness or his unworthiness.   [118

*NAACP National Convention
Los Angeles, California
July 6, 1966*

DISSENT

... There are those who feel that we may discuss too often and that we may argue too much. Let them remember that freedom is hammered out on the anvil of discussion, dissent, and debate, which ultimately yields to a decision that can be supported by the public.   [119

*Syracuse University
June 6, 1965*

... There is no party, no Chief Executive, no Cabinet, no

48

legislature in this or any other nation, wise enough to govern without constant exposure to informed criticism.   [120

Rutgers University
New Brunswick, New Jersey
September 22, 1966

... Without the right of dissent, the free debate essential to an enlightened consensus is impossible.   [121

Edward R. Murrow Center
of Public Diplomacy
Medford, Massachusetts
December 6, 1965

... "The most dangerous enemy to truth and freedom amongst us," said Ibsen, "is the compact majority." Oppose that compact majority, and you are sure to collect a few bruises. But I have found that the best remedy for a bruise is to collect a few more. The more you speak out, and the more you act, the more you are going to discover that you are lending courage to a surprising number of people whose feelings will come to the surface in response to yours.   [122

Michigan State University
East Lansing, Michigan
June 12, 1966

... Controversy and dissent are the life-blood of an active society. There are those who would wait for all the facts to come in before taking a position. Generations may die while waiting for the facts. When more facts are available you can revise or change your position.   [123

Quote Magazine
July, 1965

... The right to dissent is a sacred right. I want to warn all Americans now that one of the most precious freedoms that we have is the right to be different, yes, even the right to be obnoxiously different.   [124

Quote Magazine
September, 1966

DIXIECRATS

... A Dixiecrat is a good, conservative Republican with a Southern accent.   [125

Senate Speech
1951

·· E ··

ECONOMY

... The material needs of life are dependent on the state of our complex economic system. It is a system that Marx could not have anticipated and that today's Communists—whether partisan to Khrushchev or to Mao—fail to understand. They have long waited for our economy to falter and fail. They say that we must preach war because our economy cannot prosper in peacetime. They are wrong. We seek peace—and we know that our economy, with proper planning can meet all challenges. They will have to wait forever if they think their system can bury us. The American economic republic is the remarkable achievement of free men working together in a political democracy. The protection of freedom is the ultimate guarantee of progress. The results in our times have made the nineteenth-century achievements of the free market seem puny—and they make obsolete the Communist idea of state monopoly of economic power. Ours is the progressive system of the future; the Communists are the reactionaries.   [126

"Cause is Mankind"
Praeger

51

... The American economic miracle is the world's greatest
success story.   [127

Associated Press
New York
April 25, 1966

... We have taken modern 20th Century economics out
of the doghouse and put it into the White House. I think it
should be clear to everyone by now that it works.   [128

President's Club
New York City
January 24, 1966

... **Recessions.** I do most emphatically reject the view of
some old-fashioned economists that there must be recessions
because there always *have* been—to me, this seems as dog-
matic as Marxism.   [129

Al Smith Dinner
New York
October 13, 1965

... This country needs no more good old days like the old
days of the 1930's. It is almost impossible for your generation
to know the heartaches, the dashed hopes of the American
Depression.   [130

Huron College
Huron, South Dakota
May 31, 1966

EDUCATION

... I am deeply impressed with the value and the power of education—its value as an end in itself, its key role in the freeing of man's spirit and the enrichment of his life—and its power to shape the destinies of nations. [131

> *Fourteenth National Conference*
> *On Higher Education*
> *1959*

... Education is the keystone in the arch of man's freedom . . . If we need—as we do—to avoid the conflagrations that could consume our society, we need hearts afire with the adventure of teaching all pupils, in all neighborhoods and at all academic levels. If we need—as we do—new techniques, new instruments, and new methods to assist in the process of education, we also need something old, something eternal—the spirit of personal commitment. [132

> *White House Conference on Education*
> *July 21, 1965*

... Can we, in our wealth and power, afford the waste of a single American child? Can we find any reason for less than excellence of education and fullness of opportunity for all? I believe our educational system should know only one standard—that of excellence, whatever the location of the school building. [133

> *National Fellowship Awards Dinner*
> *Philadelphia, Pennsylvania*
> *May 23, 1966*

... The majority of Americans have come to realize that the soundest, the most productive investment a nation can make is in the education of its children.   [134

*National Association of Secondary
School Principals
Cleveland, Ohio
February 7, 1966*

... **Continuing.** The adventure of learning itself should be more broadly shared. The concept of clearly demarked school years—with the gates tightly shut after the graduate receives his diploma and returns his rented robes—is long outmoded. It does not fit into a way of life in which so many people have so much leisure, and so much interest in learning. It does not fit in an era when so much of the subject matter of learning is also the subject matter of life. The relationship of the school to the individual must be a continuing one.   [135

*Southern Conference on Education
Richmond, Virginia
December 2, 1965*

... **Dropouts.** As we concern ourselves with the problem of school dropouts, let us remember that many of these youngsters are, in fact, pushouts—persons whose unique talents are never developed or recognized by the schools—

54

persons to whom education has been a deadening and defeating experience. [136

American Personnel and
Guidance Association
Washington, D. C.
April 4, 1966

... Experience. So let us stop thinking of schooling as a product packaged in tidy little three or four year cellophane-wrapped packages. Education is experience and experience is life. The school that lives in isolation is doomed to sterility and irrelevance. [137

Southern Conference on Education
Richmond, Virginia
December 2, 1965

... Opportunity. We must make sure our young people understand that new opportunities are, in fact, opening up every day. We must crack through generations of cynicism and despair so that our boys and girls will seek the right education and training to fill the jobs of the future. [138

American Personnel and
Guidance Association
Washington, D. C.
April 4, 1966

... Opportunity. I truly hope, my young friends, that you will stay in school to brighten your path by the light of your learning—and may your learning be such that it will cast enough light to take you from where you are now into the sunlight of a brighter tomorrow.   [139

Urban League Back-To-School Rally
Washington, D. C.
August 25, 1966

...Poverty. Through investment in education we can begin to close the gap between rich and poor. Our weapons can be schoolhouses and books. Our soldiers can be teaching volunteers. Our victory can be the victory of the human spirit over hopelessness and despair. Our monument can be a society of free and creative peoples, living at peace and with the knowledge that each new day can be a better day. Let us proceed, then, to let quality in education enhance the quality of life. Let opportunity in education lend opportunity to all mankind.   [140

Public School Pre-School Conference
Cleveland, Ohio
September 7, 1965

...Poverty. Thirty-five million Americans still live in poverty; slum schools still turn out children who can't read the labels on a medicine bottle; many of the children in the Head Start program identify the Teddy bear on the chart as a rat.   [141

National Council of Churches
Miami, Florida
December 7, 1966

... **Sputnik.** I doubt that there is a school system remaining in America which has not undergone a revolution, major or minor, since Sputnik I. Sputnik hurt our national pride. It jarred us loose from our comfortable doze. And it began to get us moving. We must admit that the first Sputnik gave us a good swift kick in our complacency concerning the quality of American education. Since Sputnik I, there have been tremendous improvements in our entire educational system—of which the new mathematics and the new physics are only examples.   [142

> *San Fernando Valley State College*
> *California*
> *September 26, 1966*

... **Students.** Too often a student can emerge from a series of courses in economics and history and government without a real understanding of their interrelationship, without making the kind of synthesis that will prepare him to face and help solve the problems of his society and his nation.   [143

> *National Conference on*
> *Higher Education*
> *1959*

EDUCATION (INTERNATIONAL)

... Yesterday, we thought of the classroom as confined by four walls. Today, those walls have been opened up to the community as a whole. Tomorrow's challenge is to open them up to the wide world.   [144

DeKalb County Education Association
Atlanta, Georgia
April 29, 1966

. . . We have known for a long time that the best invest-ment we can make in America is in the education of our children. And we have come to realize that the same thing is true in the developing countries—countries seeking to raise themselves to nationhood against far greater obstacles than we in America ever faced.   [145

DeKalb County Education Association
Atlanta, Georgia
April 29, 1966

. . . This, then, is the challenge before us: Not only to educate the children of America but also to help bring edu-cation to every darkened corner where men still bend under the weight of ignorance. For it is true that freedom cannot live together with ignorance. Between the two, the choice is clear.   [146

DeKalb County Education Association
Atlanta, Georgia
April 29, 1966

EUROPE

. . . It is my belief that we stand today upon the threshold of a new era in our relations with the peoples of Europe—a period of new engagement. And I believe that this new period, if we do not lose our wits or our nerve, or our patience, can see the replacement of the Iron Curtain by the Open Door. [147

Westminster College
Fulton, Missouri
March 5, 1967

...A constructive force has been at work in Western Europe—releasing the constraining bonds of old hostilities and closed institutions to the fresh stimulation of competition and cooperation across national boundaries. That constructive force has been the will of the peoples of Western Europe that they should unite . . . Some today see Western European unity endangered by a rising wave of nationalism there. And there are those who fear that the renewal of a narrower nationalism in Western Europe must be accepted as an inevitable and immutable fact—that we must resign ourselves to the abandonment of our support for unity, and to the acceptance of a return of power politics among nations. There are a small few in other countries who conclude that the "realistic" next step toward a settlement of European problems can therefore only be by bilateral agreement between the Soviet Union and the United States—over the heads of our Western partners. I do not believe this is "realism." Neither do I believe a realistic settlement of European problems can be achieved by European nations without *our* participation, and that of the Soviet Union . . . It is precisely now—at the time when new opportunities lie

59

ahead—that we must retain cohesion with our Western partners—and they with us. If the cold war is to end, if the Iron Curtain is to be lifted, we shall need them and they will need us. [148

Westminster College
Fulton, Missouri
March 5, 1967

... The task now, in light of a new situation, is not to throw away what has been successful, but to build constructively upon it. I believe that the people of Western Europe will reject concepts of narrow nationalism and of national adventure, and will continue to move forward toward unity —toward a unified Western Europe open to expansion and conscious of its need to strengthen its ties with the nations of Eastern Europe. I believe, too, that they will reject any severing of their ties across the Atlantic—ties built firmly on common cultural heritage, on common experience, on common interest. For our part, we do not mean either to abandon our friends or to dominate them. We know that American power continues to be necessary to stability in Central Europe. We know that difficult and intractable problems—such as arms control and the reunification of Germany—must continue to involve both American and European effort . . . In our alliance, the task is this: to transform what was built on fear and common threat into a vital, working instrument built on hope and common opportunity and common responsibility. It must be an alliance *for* peace and peaceful progress, not simply *against* the spector of invasion from the East.

It must be an alliance for promotion of social and economic welfare, not simply *against* a communist threat.   [149

Westminster College
Fulton, Missouri
March 5, 1967

EXTREMISTS

... What extremist groups—both left and right—say sounds different. But what they do is similar. They share a common contempt for the democratic process and for democracy itself.   [150

National PTA Convention
Baltimore, Maryland
May 17, 1966

... I think you in the PTA can take it as something of a compliment—a right-handed compliment, so to speak—that extremist groups have in recent years chosen the PTA as a target.   [151

National PTA Convention
Baltimore, Maryland
May 17, 1966

... The outcome of the Goldwater Convention in San Francisco was a flat refusal to repudiate extremism. By its refusal to condemn the lunatic fringe of American politics,

61

the Goldwater Party has permitted into its ranks those individuals and organizations whose stock in trade is the politics of hate. [152

Fairfax County, Virginia
October 28, 1964

· · F · ·

FAMILY

... The child needs strength to lean on, a shoulder to cry on, and an example to learn from.   [153

Quote Magazine
April, 1965

... No government program, no social service, no speech by a public official is a substitute for interest at home, inspiration at home, encouragement at home.   [154

Urban League Back-To-School Rally
Washington, D. C.
August 25, 1966

... Jewish. It is the veneration for intellectual achievement which pervades the Jewish family—the tremendous pride in any child who proves capable of it—that opens the way from the humblest Jewish home to the highest peaks of excellence.   [155

Weizmann Institute Dinner
New York City
December 6, 1965

...**Negro.** Often in the back pages of our newspaper there appears the story of a Negro couple who have attained their 50th wedding anniversary, or a Negro woman who has reached the age of 100. This is their only opportunity to say to their fellow citizens what they consider most important in their lives. And, time after time, the mother will put it in some such phrase as this: "I raised five children, and none of them got into trouble." That is human dignity in its most basic form. [156

Washington University
St. Louis, Missouri
October 28, 1965

...**Negro.** We urgently need to reinforce the fragile structure of the Negro family—particularly by opening up more and better jobs for Negro men, so that they can be respected and self-respecting bread winners for their own families. [157

Washington University
St. Louis, Missouri
October 28, 1965

...**Welfare.** Public welfare must seek to strengthen and preserve the family unit. It must take a leading role in the attack on such problems as dependency, juvenile delinquency, family breakdown, illegitimacy, ill health and disability. [158

Washington University
St. Louis, Missouri
October 28, 1965

FOOD FOR PEACE

... When President Truman looked out on a turbulent, impoverished and hungry world in 1949, he had little immediate hope that this nation—and our partners—would in his lifetime be able to challenge those conditions. But today we are able to challenge them—and we are able to do so in large part because of the energy and productivity of American agriculture. Today our abundance is a weapon for peace. We must use that weapon—ably, honorably, and well.   [159

Mid-Continent Farmers' Association
Columbia, Missouri
August 8, 1966

... This country has large international responsibilities which it cannot and must not shirk. We are committed to our friends and our allies and our food and fiber supplies must be adequate to meet all foreseeable needs. It is important that we maintain an arsenal of food and fiber, just as we maintain an arsenal of weapons. Both serve the cause of freedom and peace.   [160

American Agricultural
Editors' Association
Washington, D. C.
June 22, 1966

... **Food Power.** In the long run, our food power—far more than military power—can be the critical factor in the achievement both of democratic institutions and of safety in the world. Food power is our secret weapon. Food is life. Food is strength. Food is hope and compassion. Food is the giver of health and vigor to children. Food is the vital ingredient of social stability and peaceful change. Let us use that power wisely and well. [161

National Grange
Minneapolis, Minnesota
November 18, 1966

... I believe one of our most powerful weapons for peace is our food power. There is still abroad in the land the general impression that we are a nation of bulging granaries and gigantic farm surpluses—a nation with a clumsy embarrassment of agricultural riches. This is not true today. It will be less true tomorrow. The surplus today is a surplus of hunger. We must do everything we can to defeat hunger or we shall soon have a surplus of trouble. [162

Buffalo Club
Buffalo, New York
January 6, 1967

FOREIGN POLICY

... Foreign policy is really domestic policy with its hat on. [163

United States Junior
Chamber of Commerce
Detroit, Michigan
June 29, 1966

... We urgently need to design and launch a broad-gauged and affirmative foreign policy on the natural

66

strengths of our nation—yes, to harness to the plow of foreign policy our tremendous industrial capacity, our abundant capital, our technical knowledge, our agricultural abundance, our wealth of trained educators, agriculturists, administrators, technicians, doctors and students.   [164

*National Conference on
Higher Education
1959*

... Change. Hubert Humphrey is no "status quo" man. He is for change—change to meet the needs and priorities of the times. And I believe our foreign policy has, above all, met the need for change while still remaining true both to principle and national self-interest.   [165

*National Governors Conference
Los Angeles, California
July 6, 1966*

... Reality. You cannot escape reality. Trouble in little nations can be the downfall of large nations.   [166

*Quote Magazine
March, 1965*

... The Record. In the past 20 years we have provided some 120 billion dollars of assistance to others. In the past 20 years our armed forces have suffered more than 165 thousand casualties on foreign soil. We have not done these things as conquerors or empire-builders. We have not done them for commercial advantage or to establish spheres of influence. We have done them because to have done otherwise would have been to deny what President Kennedy called "the ideals of honor and faith we inherit from our forefathers, the decency of purpose, steadfastness of resolve and strength of will, the courage and the humility which they possessed." [167

Texas Christian University
Forth Worth, Texas
July 15, 1966

FREE SOCIETY

... A free society requires more than power and wealth. It must be based on justice and opportunity. The modern industrialized nation needs, too, a sense of concern—that sense, if you will, of heightened moral sensibility which stems from the arts and humanities. We need a society of compassion as well as comfort, of humanism as well as hardware, of freedom as well as food. [168

St. John's University
Collegeville, Minnesota
May 7, 1966

... A totalitarian state can offer total security. But only an open society can offer its citizens the freedom to seek self-fulfillment—and that, I think, is the real meaning of happiness. [169

University of Chicago
January 14, 1966

FREEDOM

... Freedom to worship God in our own way means tolerating those who believe differently than we do, those who think by different lights, and who, perhaps, express different values. It means that the security of our own beliefs will not feel threatened by other voices or other views. Freedom of speech and expression means coping with a people who are informed, critical, inquiring and, yes, sometimes opposed to the policies of their government. It means that the voice of the people shall be heard, whether the voice is pleasing to those in power or not. Freedom from want means that a government of the people shall harness national wealth and resources to insure its citizens access to the essentials of life. Freedom from fear means creating a secure and humane society that will enrich the human spirit, not smother it with oppressive conformity or tyrannical pressures. Freedom from fear means the freedom to be—fully and completely—a human being responsive to the challenges of our time. [170

Italian-American Labor Council
New York City
December 17, 1966

... The strongest bulwark of liberty is man, free and in search of himself. [171

Michigan State University
East Lansing, Michigan
June 12, 1966

... Modern man is not ruled by political dogma. The great moving force in the world today is humanity's craving

69

for freedom, for opportunity, for a fuller share of the blessings of life—above all, for a chance for individual expression and fulfillment—in short, for the very things which lie at the heart of our American Revolution. [172

> *United States Junior*
> *Chamber of Commerce*
> *Detroit, Michigan*
> *June 29, 1966*

. . . Personal Responsibility. Each of you must assume a personal responsibility for preserving freedom in these perilous times. This is not the business of someone else; it is your business. Freedom is the personal commitment and responsibility of each and every one. [173

> *Syracuse University*
> *June 6, 1965*

. . . Revolution. The marching feet in the world today are those of people seeking freedom. [174

> *United States Junior*
> *Chamber of Commerce,*
> *Detroit, Michigan*
> *June 29, 1966*

. . . Self-Discovery. True freedom in any land is a relentless, never ending process of self-discovery among its people. [175

> *Michigan State University*
> *East Lansing, Michigan*
> *June 12, 1966*

... **Vitality.**   It is the atmosphere of freedom which gives American life its enormous vitality, its magnificent promise.
[176

New York City
October 29, 1964

FUTURE

... As recently as 1930, even so towering a genius as Albert Einstein could say about the future: "I never think of it. It comes soon enough." Today, the future rushes toward us far too quickly for comfort. We can no longer "Seize the day!" as the poet Horace counseled, for today has become little more than a faint blur between yesterday and tomorrow . . . It took mankind 200,000 years to emerge from the Stone Age. It took another 10,000 years from the first use of metal tools to the Industrial Revolution, now hardly a century old. Two key exhibits in our Smithsonian Institution vividly illustrate the dramatic acceleration in the tempo of progress. One is the first commercial computer, only 17 years old. The other is astronaut John Glenn's space capsule, only four years old, but already a museum piece . . . It is no wonder that the future has ceased to be the domain of oracles and astrologers, and become a serious preoccupation of scholars, government officials, and businessmen. For, to the extent that we can foresee the future, we may be able to achieve some control over it.   [177

University of Minnesota at Duluth
June 10, 1966

... In 1946, after a long and full life, the poet Gertrude

71

Stein lay dying in Paris. An old friend of hers came to her bedside, anxious to grasp the wisdom of a lifetime before it slipped away. "Gertrude," the friend said, "what is the answer?" Miss Stein replied, "what is the question?" The American who looks ahead today faces a somewhat similar dilemma. Not only don't we have answers, but even the questions sometimes seem hard to figure out.   [178

United Jewish Appeal
New York City
December 10, 1966

. . . And Past. Every generation has heard its false prophets pleading for a return to the glories of yesterday, only thereby to sacrifice their right to participate in the building of today and tomorrow.   [179

National Association of Counties
Washington, D. C.
August 12, 1964

. . . "Good Old Days." The good old days were never that good, believe me. The good new days are today. And better days are coming tomorrow.   [180

American Personnel and
Guidance Association
April 4, 1966

FUTURE (AMERICA)

. . . Life in our cities can be more than steaming asphalt and crowded tenements, more than filthy air and polluted water, more than clogged highways and congested streets, more than bursting schoolrooms and underpaid teachers, more than violence and hopelessness and discrimination and hate and despair, more than temporary material satisfaction . . . The way lies open to build a society in which the human values, above all, count uppermost. The way lies open to cities filled with green and open space, to transportation that is safe, comfortable, rapid, to neighborhoods once more filled with neighbors, to schools and universities that truly care about the future of our children, to rural areas, towns, cities, suburbs where people—because they are citizens, because they are people—can live together in harmony and cooperation, no matter what their age, the color of their skin, their religion, or their last name.   [181

Democratic State Convention
Buffalo, New York
September 8, 1966

. . . History may be against us, but I believe the cause of justice is with us. It is with us when we say to the Negro: "Here is a ballot that gives you full citizenship, after promises broken for a hundred years." It is with us when we say to the poor: "Here is hope where there has been no hope." It is with us when we say to every American: "We can have a land of goodness, of beauty, of culture, and of opportunity."   [182

Women's Democratic Conference
Washington, D. C.
April 18, 1966

... Sometimes the good news and the record of achievement are obscured by a poor choice of words, or confusing headlines. So let me make one or two things clear. If things are better today than yesterday, we nevertheless seek to make them even better tomorrow. We are a restless people, and we seek higher standards and higher goals all the time.   [183

American Agricultural
Editors' Association
Washington, D. C.
June 22, 1966

... If we still have a long way to go, and we have in achieving human equality, in securing international and domestic tranquillity, in extending the benefits of our technical genius to all citizens in the American republic and to all mankind, let us at least glorify in and be inspired by the magnitude of the unfinished agenda. Let us glory in the fact that we still possess the wit and the wisdom to continue making our American democratic system responsive to the terribly difficult and complex problems of this turbulent and rapidly changing age.   [184

Syracuse University
June 6, 1965

FUTURE (WORLD)

... It has been my privilege, with your help, to play a role in the drama of American democratic action for over two decades. We've come a long way together and we've been through a good many battles. But *tomorrow* will always be the time for us. Tomorrow could be a cataclysm of nuclear destruction. Or tomorrow can be the opening of a bright new era of human freedom and expression. If we keep our wits about us, if we hold our nerve, if we never cease working, we can have a world of brotherhood and peace—the world we've dreamed of.

[185

National Convention
Americans for Democratic Action
Washington, D. C.
April 23, 1966

... May the blessing of your generation be the opportunity to help build a world in which men may dwell in homes of light, in valleys green with nature's bounty, in nations ruled by laws of justice, and in the knowledge that, for their children, there lie ahead uplands of opportunity and freedom for the human spirit.

[186

Huron College
Huron, South Dakota
May 31, 1966

... I believe there is a movement in history. I believe it is a movement in the right direction. I believe it is a movement which points in the direction of man's freedom and liberation—a movement in which self-determination and peaceful development will be the strongest single influences. We have rid ourselves of excess baggage. The colonial period is behind us. If we maintain our cohesion, the period of the cold war can be behind us. And a whole new era of opportunity can lie ahead . . . My business is politics. Yet the business of politics is more than practicality. It is the business of looking ahead. It is the business, if you will permit, of vision. Such a vision today must be a human vision, a world vision—not an exclusive American one, if it is to light the future and give men hope . . . It is not given to any single one of us to see the vision in all its clarity. But the vision is there. It is the task of each of us to help make it visible and then to translate it into reality. [187

Bonn, Germany
April, 1967

·· G ··

GOLDWATER, BARRY

... Senator Goldwater is a decent private citizen, a man
you would welcome as your neighbor, but he is clearly
unqualified for the high office of President of the United
States. [188

Los Angeles, California
October 31, 1964

GOVERNMENT

... America is a big country, with big problems and bigger
opportunities. It cannot afford a little government, a government unequal to its responsibilities. [189

University of Chicago
January 14, 1966

... There is a new spirit today in the government of the
United States. Not a spirit of harrassment; not a spirit of
doubt and suspicion of what you're trying to do, Mr. Businessman or Mr. Labor; but rather a spirit of seeing whether
we can't work together and learn from you and ask for your

77

help to bring this nation to new heights of strength and
power and of justice.   [190

Economic Club of Detroit
October 22, 1965

... You know that a government that cares about the
unfortunate and the afflicted is a government that deserves
your respect. You know that compassion is not weakness and
that concern for the unfortunate is not socialism.   [191

Democratic State Convention
Little Rock, Arkansas
September 18, 1964

GOVERNMENT (FEDERALISM)

... Creative federalism means programs, policies, and projects locally inspired, locally developed, locally administered—but with a broader design that includes state and
regional development, backed and supported by federal assistance and resources.   [192

Urban America Conference
Washington, D. C.
September 13, 1966

... We in Washington don't see state and local governments as rivals of the federal government—we see them as
working partners in the service of one boss, the American
people.   [193

University of Chicago
January 14, 1966

... American government is more than Washington. American government is Washington, the state capital, the county court houses, the city and village halls, the town meetings and the thousands of commissions and local school boards.

[194

Democratic State Convention
Little Rock, Arkansas
September 18, 1964

... There are very few problems in America that are purely state problems, or purely city problems, or purely rural problems. There are enough problems, enough challenges, enough opportunities in today's and tomorrow's America to keep us all hard at work—and we shall do much better working together than separately or even against one another.

[195

Conference of State
Legislative Leaders
Washington, D. C.
November 19, 1966

GOVERNMENT (LOCAL)

... Today our country faces a crisis of *local* government because our urban areas no longer remotely resemble what they were at the turn of the century. The services people need—and the revenues needed to pay for them—just can't be provided in the mixed-up, overlapping, outdated framework built around, over and through our metropolitan areas. In city after city I visit, I find mayors without authority, city

79

treasuries without money, and anywhere from 10 to a thousand jurisdictions trying to run things.   [196

Convention, United Steelworkers
of America
Atlantic City, New Jersey
September 23, 1966

. . . It is in state houses, city halls, and local town meetings—not the halls of Congress or the federal courtrooms —where the major battles of the next phase of the civil rights struggle will be waged. It is in our states and local communities where we must wage the war against slumism.

[197

White House Conference
"To Fulfill These Rights"
June 1, 1966

GREAT SOCIETY

. . . The Great Society is not the old-fashioned welfare state, redistributing from above the limited resources of a static economy. It is the opportunity state, seeking to give every citizen the same means to realize his full potentialities, and thus to advance and enliven the community generally.

[198

University of Chicago
January 14, 1966

. . . We will have our Great Society one day. And when it's finished we'll have a society where there is a joy of living, a life of purpose. A society young of spirit and young of heart, but mature in mind. A society with love of children, and with respect for its elders. A society which works for education and strives for human dignity. A society where everyone—black, white, young, old, man, woman,—*everyone* is important. A society where culture and beauty are a main course and not a dessert. A society where everyone is productive and a full participant in American life.   [199

Women's Democratic Conference
Washington, D. C.
April 18, 1966

... There are those who charge today that the Great Society—and the legislation enacted to implement it—represents a great extension of federal activity and power. But this is not the case. The key elements of the Great Society were not plucked out of thin air in Washington. Rather, they are goals for which men and women of good will—and organizations of good will—have been working and fighting for over many years.   [200

University of Chicago
January 14, 1966

··H··

HERESY AND PROPHECY

... The difference between heresy and prophecy is often one of sequence. Heresy often turns out to have been prophecy—when properly aged.　　　　　　　　　　　　[201

> *National Convention*
> *Americans for Democratic Action*
> *Washington, D. C.*
> *April 23, 1966*

HISTORY

... The course of history is not a mindless juggernaut we are powerless to control, but a fresh challenge susceptible to courageous action in each generation.　　　　　　[202

> *Michigan State University*
> *East Lansing, Michigan*
> *June 12, 1966*

... You can get a good many frustrations out of your

system by cursing history. But cursing history is no substitute for facing the options that exist today.   [203

National Governors Conference
Los Angeles, California
July 6, 1966

... **Perspective.**   History has a way of shrinking to proper size the episodes which capture the public's attention for a fleeting moment. And it has a way of raising to proper size the acts of wisdom, of vision, and of courage.   [204

White House Conference
"To Fulfill These Rights"
June 1, 1966

HUMAN DIGNITY

... Either we recognize and practice the basic principles of our moral and political faith—the dignity of the individual, freedom of conscience, and the brotherhood of mankind—or we forfeit the privilege of freedom and the claim to decency.   [205

Address as State Chief of
  War Service Section
Minnesota Work Projects Administration
At the Annual Conference of
  the Minnesota Library Association
October 1, 1942

... There is, in short, an urgent need to build a new climate of mutual respect among all elements of society. For it is this absence of respect—and the sense of responsibility which is engendered by respect—which lies at the roots of the hostility and suspicion which today threatens the tranquillity and progress of some cities.   [206

White House Conference
"To Fulfill These Rights"
June 1, 1966

... A truly humanized life consists of more than merely possessing adequate food and shelter. We know it involves primarily the chance to use the unique spiritual qualities which man alone possesses—the ability to create, to judge, to exercise freedom, to accept responsibility and to acquire dignity and self-respect.   [207

National Catholic Social
Action Conference
Georgetown University
Washington, D. C.
August 26, 1966

... **Relief.** We must defend the human dignity of the recipients of relief, and we shall continue to do so. But I am glad to say that we have turned the corner, and are putting our major stress on positive steps to enhance dignity and self-respect—including getting those who are potentially employable off relief and into the mainstream of American economy.   [208

Washington University
St. Louis, Missouri
October 28, 1965

HUMAN RIGHTS (INTERNATIONAL)

. . . Human rights are not a danger or even a luxury. They are essential to the dignity of every human being—and to the well-being and progress of nations as well. They are not burdens to be reluctantly shouldered, but opportunities to be confidently and gladly grasped. I predict that, as governments move towards assuring their citizens their full human rights, they will reap—as we have here in America—a rich reward. They will set off a veritable ferment of initiative and creativity. For there are incalculable resources in the human spirit, once it has been set free. All of us, as we grew up, had to learn not to be afraid of the dark. As peoples and as governments mature, *they* must learn not to be afraid of the light. [209

Adas Israel Synagogue
Washington, D. C.
December 10, 1966

. . . Human rights are what the big foreign policy issues of our time are really all about—because a belief in the worth and dignity of every individual is what distinguishes the United States and its allies from the totalitarian countries of the right and of the left. If we have been, and are, powerful in the world, it is not only because our country is a storehouse of goods and an arsenal of weapons, but also because we offer hope to all who seek to realize the rights and dignity of man. [210

"Race in a Changing World"
American Jewish Committee

86

HUMANITIES

... There is an abundance of specialists who can provide us with the facts relevant to decisions—the "what," the "where," the "when," and the "how," but when they have laid their facts upon the table, an essential factor is still missing: The "why." But no narrow specialty or expertise can provide the full and essential group of the continuity of past, present and future that the humanities do.   [211

American Council of Learned Societies
Washington, D. C.
January 20, 1966

IDEAS

... The power of an idea, the courage that comes through reasoned understanding, these are the intangible, the secret weapons of a free people.   [212

> *Address as State Chief of*
> *War Services Section*
> *Minnesota Work Projects Administration*
> *At the Annual Conference of*
> *the Minnesota Library Association*
> *October 1, 1942*

... The true source of our national power is our power of intellect—of our wealth, our wealth of ideas—of our resources, our resources of human skill and energy.   [213

> *Southern Conference on Education*
> *Richmond, Virginia*
> *December 2, 1965*

IMMIGRANTS

... Fortunately, the time has long passed when people

liked to regard the United States as some kind of melting pot, taking men and women from every part of the world and converting them into standardized, homogenized Americans. We are, I think, much more mature and wise today. Just as we welcome a world of diversity, so we glory in an America of diversity—an America all the richer for the many different and distinctive strands of which it is woven.   [214

All-America Tribute to
Archbishop Iakovos
Chicago, Illinois
January 15, 1967

INDIA

... Throughout the years, India has maintained the basic freedoms of speech, of the press, and of assembly. The people have been free to elect their representatives and free to reject them as well—and they have vigorously exercised both freedoms. They have hewed steadfastly to the democratic way—in the short run, perhaps, the most demanding way, but in the long run the most rewarding.   [215

Memorial Service for
Prime Minister Shastri
Washington Cathedral
January 28, 1966

INDIVIDUALISM

... The great challenge which faces us is to assure that, in our society of bigness, we do not strangle the voice of creativity, that the rules of the game do not come to overshadow its purpose, that the grand orchestration of society leaves ample room for the man who marches to the music of another drummer. [216

*United States Junior
    Chamber of Commerce
Detroit, Michigan
June 29, 1966*

... The word "individualism" itself was invented by one of our earliest and most perceptive foreign observers, Alexis de Tocqueville, to describe the spirit he found already prevalent in America over a century ago. I know that there are many young people who fear that, in this age of big government, big business, big labor—and big universities too—we are in danger of being reduced to numbers and converted into fodder for computers. On one college campus, in fact, I recently saw students with placards saying: "I am a human being—do not fold, staple or mutilate!" I know that you, of all people, are determined not to be standardized or homogenized. For you have learned from your own early experience a basic truth. Governments don't have ideas; companies don't have ideas; laboratories don't have ideas. And—contrary to a popular myth—computers don't have ideas. People have ideas. And not people in the mass, but individual human beings. [217

*Science Talent Search
    Awards Banquet
Washington, D. C.
March 6, 1967*

... **Responsibility.** The individual cannot shrug his shoulders and withdraw to his television opiate, leaving decisions and matters of individual concern to others. To do so would be to guarantee the weakening of our democratic system and the victory of faceless impersonality, and to leave the field to change unharnessed and unchanneled. For all the actions in the world by governments—federal, state, and local —and by the private institutions within our society will be fruitless if they are done *to* the individual citizen instead of *with* and *by* him. Individual responsibility and individual participation—these are the most effective antidotes to "alienation," "estrangement," "dehumanization," and all the other phenomena which are beginning to so much concern us.   [218

University of West Virginia
Morgantown, West Virginia
October 7, 1966

ISOLATIONISM

... Either we cast aside our political isolationism, or we must prepare for a more devastating conflict. Either we cast aside our indifference to the fate of other people, or these "other people" will threaten our own security.   [219

Address as State Chief of
War Services Section
Minnesota Work Projects Administration
At the Annual Conference of the
Minnesota Library Association
October 1, 1942

. . . In today's world, no man, no nation, can remain isolated from the affairs of others. [220

University of California
Berkeley, California
October 5, 1964

. . . National isolation breeds national neurosis. [221

Buffalo Club
Buffalo, New York
January 6, 1967

. . . I've been reading back through old newspapers. Some
of the same people who say we have no business in Asia
today were saying, in 1939, that we had no business in
Europe. Some of the same people who say we have no
business in Vietnam today were saying, in 1948, that we had
no business in Greece—in 1950, that we had no business in
Korea. [222

Democratic Campaign Conference
Washington, D. C.
July 27, 1966

ISRAEL

. . . The people of Israel have truly made the desert blos-
som. The spirit is so contagious that, when you visit there,
you want to roll up your sleeves and get to work too. [223

Truman Award Banquet
Kansas City, Missouri
December 19, 1965

JAPAN

... In Japan we have a staunch friend, a highly developed nation, our second trading partner, an immense potential force for the development of Asia.   [224

West Point, New York
June 8, 1966

JOHNSON, LYNDON B.

... I pay tribute to the President of the United States, who has done more than any man that I know of to preach a doctrine of understanding and of cooperation in this country; a man that knows no North or South or East or West, but knows the United States of America.   [225

Economic Club of Detroit
October 22, 1965

... President Johnson is a man with the instincts of a teacher, who would rather persuade than compel, who would rather unite than divide.   [226

Acceptance Address
Democratic Convention
August 28, 1964

·· K ··

KENNEDY, JOHN F.

... John F. Kennedy will be recorded in the annals of history as one who by dedicated action contributed much to the achievement of equal rights—not because it was good politics, but because it was right.   [227

"Integration vs. Segregation"
Crowell

... The President (Kennedy) has converted his political popularity into political power. That's what popularity is for. It's like money in the bank. It's to be used.   [228

Interview
1961

· · L · ·

LABOR

... Union organizations have provided for millions of formerly inarticulate citizens the forum in which to hammer out policies affecting the world in which they live and which their children will inherit. And not only have they hammered out policies, but they have developed techniques and resources for implementing those policies. That is what I find so right about the labor movement. Unions have made democracy and citizenship and the right to petition a reality to millions of men and women.   [229

"Cause is Mankind"
Praeger

LATIN AMERICA

... The new era in relations between the United States and Latin America which President Kennedy opened—and President Johnson continues—is based on understanding and respect for Latin American people, for their culture and many of their traditions. It is based on an acceptance of Latin American people as equals and on a recognition that

99

the United States has much to learn from Latin American nations. [230

Tucson, Arizona
November 1, 1964

... The Alliance for Progress is a bold challenge to those who cry, with communists and other extremists, that mankind cannot be freed from its bonds of ignorance and poverty without the violent destruction of the existing system and the imposition of a dictatorship. It is a cooperative venture undertaken in the belief that the processes of constitutional democracy can move sufficiently swiftly and decisively to accomplish vital, urgent social and economic changes. I am committed to the proposition, and this nation is committed to the proposition, that change—radical, revolutionary change—can come through orderly, peaceful processes. [231

"Cause is Mankind"
Praeger

... Perfecting political democracy and strengthening constitutional government are an essential part of the Alliance for Progress. Where political leadership has been strong, democratic institutions have survived. But there is no doubt that progress in preserving and extending democratic political institutions has at best been uneven. There have been recent hopeful signs—such as the peaceful transfers of power in Venezuela, Chile, Costa Rica, Guatemala, Colombia, and the Dominican Republic. In other countries military *coups d'etat*—not free elections—have brought changes in

100

the government. Until ways are found to strengthen the political fabric of Latin societies . . . to perfect the institutions which are the sub-structure of a stable political system, we cannot be sure that military *coups d'etat* represent only a temporary aberration and not a permanent trend.   [232

Operation Amigo Dinner
Pan-American Union
Washington, D. C.
November 10, 1966

LAW AND ORDER

. . . The vital task of building a system of justice that treats all people alike, black and white, rich and poor, must be carried out in our cities, in our towns and countries. "Equal justice under law" is more than a slogan etched on the entrance of the Supreme Court.   [233

NAACP National Convention
Los Angeles, California
July 6, 1966

. . . **Individual Responsibility.**   In a democracy such as ours, the preservation of law and order begins with the individual. Within the limit of his capabilities, every American has an obligation not only to uphold the law, but to support it with all reasonable means at his command.   [234

Graduation Exercises
FBI National Academy
Washington, D. C.
May 25, 1966

. . . Individual Responsibility. When the buck stops in the preservation of law and order, it stops in front of every citizen. And it will take nothing less than the effort and understanding of every citizen to bring us through to a time when neighbor lives in peace with neighbor, when law observance is the rule and law enforcement is the exception, when every American community stands equally committed to civil peace and to social justice. [235

International Association of
Chiefs of Police
Philadelphia, Pennsylvania
October 5, 1966

. . . Law Enforcement Officers. I want Americans young and old, to trust and respect the man with the badge—not merely because he wears it, but because he wears it with honor. [236

Graduation Exercises
FBI National Academy
Washington, D. C.
May 25, 1966

. . . Police-Community Relations. We find, time and again, that in those cities where police-community relations are best, police officers are associated with the United Fund, with athletics, with church activity, with recreation programs for children and young adults. Our police officers should be given more time in the schools to talk about law enforcement, to explain their work, to identify with young people—and to have young people identify with them. [237

*International Association
of Chiefs of Police
Philadelphia, Pennsylvania
October 5, 1966*

... **Violence.** There is a basic and obvious difference between peaceful demonstration and non-violent protest and brutal, uncontrolled, destructive hoodlumism and rioting. The wanton destruction of property, gangsterism, arson, and gunfire will only destroy the framework of justice and law we are laboring to build. No responsible public official can condone violence any more in Los Angeles than in Mississippi.   [238

*National Student Association
University of Wisconsin
August 23, 1965*

... **War on Poverty.** The war on poverty is being administered to eradicate the stagnant pools of bitterness and frustration which breed much of our present-day crime.   [239

*Graduation Exercises
FBI National Academy
Washington, D. C.
May 25, 1966*

LIBERALISM

... The enduring strength of American liberalism is that it recognizes and welcomes change as an essential part of life, and moves to seize rather than evade the challenges and opportunities that change presents. It is, basically, an attitude toward life rather than a dogma—characterized by a warm heart, an open mind, and willing hands. Without a warm heart, it would lack its essential sensitivity and responsiveness to the needs and aspirations of people at home and abroad. Without an open mind, it would lack its essential ability to recognize new problems and think through new solutions. Without the willingness to act, and to act boldly, it would lack its characteristic ability to translate feelings and thoughts into meaningful deeds. That is why I am proud to be a modern American liberal, ever conscious of the great achievements of our past, ever confident about our future.

[240

"The Cause Is Mankind"
Praeger

... One conviction of American liberalism is that people must speak for themselves, and liberals should rejoice whenever people are able to speak for themselves; because liberalism, above all, means emancipation—emancipation from one's fears, his inadequacies, from prejudice, from discrimination, yes, from poverty.

Liberalism also means opportunity—not just opportunity in word, but opportunity in the fact of life—the opportunity to be a meaningful participant in all the affairs of life. It means self-respect that is gained by self-help, and it means human-dignity that comes from being a respected citizen with full and equal rights.

Another conviction of American liberalism is this: that the voice of the disinherited can be heard and social justice can be attained, within the institutions of American society, within the framework of the rule of law, of the constitution, of consensus and democratic practice and processes.

Our institutions are built for change; they include within them the principles of self-criticism, of expansion, and of improvement towards a higher justice . . .

But now I must quickly add another conviction of American liberalism, that the job is never done, and it takes unremitting effort and persevering patience. It would be an historic tragedy if we thought our work was done and if we stopped now.

Too many Americans seem to believe that having passed the four Civil Rights Acts of the past ten years, we have shown our good intentions and have done enough. In fact, some people say we should pause, that we should relax. I don't think so. Too many Americans seem to think that having started a wide variety of anti-poverty programs we have done enough.

They say it's time to re-group our forces, to hold for a while, yes, to pause when, in fact, it is just time now to move into action. But, the real test is not how many laws we have passed or how many programs we have begun, but how many people have been helped and how many people still need help. [241

Freedom House
New York City
March 29, 1967

LIFE (VALUE OF)

. . . I wish that as much emphasis were placed on the lives

that we save as is placed on the lives that are lost because of war. [242

American Agricultural
Editors' Association
Washington, D. C.
June 22, 1966

... We value life. Life is precious. The hardy men and women who built this country stood firm for the principle that man's freedom and independence were worth the risk of life—yes, worth the risk of life, fortune and sacred honor. [243

*Texas Christian University
Fort Worth, Texas
July 15, 1966*

... When a nation sends its young men to war, it must be sure indeed that the cause is worth the terrible cost. [244

*Arlington Memorial Cemetery
November 11, 1965*

$\cdot\cdot$ M $\cdot\cdot$

MILITARY POWER

... Our "doves" must learn that there are times when power must be used. They must learn that there is no substitute for force in the face of a determined enemy who resorts to terror, subversion and aggression, whether concealed or open. Our "hawks" must learn that military power is not enough. They must learn, indeed, that it can be wholly unavailing if not accompanied by political effort and by the credible promise to ordinary people of a better life.

[245

West Point
June 8, 1966

·· N ··

NATIONAL PURPOSE

... Education, medical care, war against poverty, programs of retraining and redevelopment, better cities and transportation, an even more productive agriculture—yes, equality at the ballot box and before the law—these are the most basic investments of all in an America able to keep its commitments both at home and abroad.

We must build an America so strong, so free, so able to lead, that there may be no question about our purpose or our endurance. Basic to this is the necessity of building an economy of growth and opportunity, yet stable in times when it is tested.   [246

University of Florida
Gainesville, Florida
October 28, 1966

... A good share of America—a share approaching a majority—is today a society in search of a motive, a society in search of a question that leads to a purposeful answer. With a firm purpose, we are everything. But irresolute, malcontent, aimless, we can become very little, very quickly.   [247

United Jewish Appeal
New York City
December 19, 1966

...We are not complacent. We do not aspire to be an island of contentment in the midst of a stormy sea. Ahead of us lies the ageless dream of man—a dream common to both the cultures of Italy and America: To live a useful and productive life in freedom and dignity.   [248

Italian-American Labor Council
New York City
December 17, 1966

...We seek not to paralyze initiative, but to revive it; not to build up the opportunity of those below at the expense of those above, but to broaden the horizons of both; not to dictate the terms of help, but to allow each community to find its own answers in its own way.   [249

United States Junior
  Chamber of Commerce
Detroit, Michigan
June 29, 1966

NATO

...For almost a generation, aggression in Europe has been deterred. But NATO has been more than a shield of protection. It has been a wellspring of confidence and security giving impetus to prosperity and progress, to economic growth and political cooperation. [250

NATO Parliamentarians
New York City
October 5, 1965

NEGRO HISTORY

... One of the great tragedies of America has been that so few persons appreciate or even know the remarkable contributions of Negroes to this Nation's history. I call upon the schools of America, public and private, to make known to the young people of this land, in coming generations, the story of the contributions of the American Negro to the American Republic. What a glorious chapter! Negroes have been a part of America since Jamestown. They suffered and survived the cruel yoke of slavery. They have experienced hardship and discrimination of a severity and duration that no other group of Americans has ever known. [251

NAACP National Convention
Los Angeles, California
July 6, 1966

NEWSPAPERS

... I know that, for you editors, choice is necessary and inevitable. You must choose what stories should be written, how they should be written, and whether they should be played up or down. I would suggest, in all humility, that fanning the flames of racial or religious prejudice—however unwittingly—is highly dangerous in a society based on the dignity of man. I would suggest that religious labeling is as undesirable as racial labeling. Let's talk programs and quit exploring prejudices.   [252

*American Society of
Newspaper Editors
Washington, D. C.
April 21, 1960*

. . . I know that all of us in government sometimes doubt just how much we are governing; but few of us doubt the influence of newspapers, or, for that matter, the men and women who manage and produce them. If any of you underestimate your influence, I suggest you consult with Mrs. Humphrey some morning, just after I've finished reading the editorial pages—and gone storming out of our apartment.   [253

*International Newspaper
Advertising Executives
Washington, D. C.
January 26, 1967*

. . . It is always a risk to speak to the press: they are likely to report what you say.   [254

*Associated Press
New York
April 25, 1966*

NIEBUHR, REINHOLD

... The 1920's and early '30's were empty years in American intellectual and political life. It was into this moral vacuum that a new voice was heard—the voice of an unknown preacher serving a working class community in Detroit. Ever since that time, Reinhold Niebuhr has been taming cynics and pulling utopians back to earth. No preacher in our time has had a greater impact on a secular world. No American has made a greater contribution to political wisdom and moral responsibility. Reinhold Niebuhr, like Abraham Lincoln and Mark Twain, came out of that great Middlewestern river valley, and he brought East with him realism and humor and energy and a brooding thoughtfulness. Like Lincoln and Mark Twain, Dr. Niebuhr brought a mixture of profundity and practicality. Like Lincoln, who I think has always been his favorite statesman, Dr. Niebuhr showed how to combine *decisive action* with a *sensitive knowledge of the complexity of life,* including politics. [255

> *"Christianity and Crisis"*
> *25th Anniversary*
> *New York*
> *February 25, 1966*

NIXON, RICHARD M.

... Some people say he will be a hard man to beat but I say, between the low road and the high road, the old model and the new model, the juvenile delinquent and the statesman, he may be a hard man to find. [256

> *Speech*
> *1960 Campaign*

· · O · ·

OPPORTUNITY

... It is this inability to choose—this denial of the right to chart one's destiny or to be a real participant in the social, economic or political life of this country—which produces the frustration, the bitterness, hopelessness and outrage we encounter today in the urban ghettoes of America. To assure each human being a chance to choose—to become everything that he is capable of becoming—this is what the American democratic system is all about. And we can never rest until *every* American has this opportunity.   [257

> *National Convention*
> *Americans for Democratic Action*
> *Washington, D. C.*
> *April 23, 1966*

... We are not avoiding Owellian misery by constructing a welfare utopia that would diminish human choice and incentive. Instead, we seek a course that provides growth, purpose and direction to all who are willing to grasp the chance to use their talents and energy. Our system does not guarantee individual success. But it can—and does—provide the climate and opportunity for the individual to be himself and to go as far as his abilities allow.   [258

> *United States Junior*
> *Chamber of Commerce*
> *Detroit, Michigan*
> *June 29, 1966*

... Our goal is to bring into being here in the United States not a handout state or even a welfare state, but a state of opportunity.   [259

> *National PTA Convention*
> *Baltimore, Maryland*
> *May 17, 1966*

... We are united in our determination to accomplish something that no nation has previously dared to try: to make every citizen in our society a full and productive member *of* our society.   [260

> *Associated Press*
> *New York*
> *April 25, 1966*

··P··

PARENTS

... It may be very hard to believe but, in another century's history books, the very people who have been helping with your tuition may be ranked among the greatest radicals of modern history. Some of your parents might flinch if you told them there were radicals in your family. But they have been nothing less.

Theirs is the first generation in all history which, by its own hand, has surrendered the privilege of telling its offspring: This is how things are; this is how they have always been; this is the way the world goes.

Your fathers and mothers were born children of hills and valleys. Today, they see the galaxy itself. They have created amazing new systems of management, science and technology. They have fought and won wars. They have designed and created international political and economic institutions that they hoped might help keep the peace. They have revitalized an economy that was faltering and made it vibrant and successful. They have found new and better systems to care for people. [261]

Michigan State University
East Lansing, Michigan
June 12, 1966

117

PEACE

... Our commitment to strengthening the peace has not weakened. We seek a peace that is more than a pause between wars. But our knowledge of ourselves tells us that we can expect no sudden epidemic of peace, that we have far to go before, as President Johnson says, the "greatness of our institutions" matches the "grandeur of our intentions." The pursuit of peace is a gradual process.

Peace is too important to be the exclusive concern of the great powers. It requires the attention of all—small nations and large, old nations and new.

The pursuit of peace resembles the building of a great cathedral. It is the work of a generation. In concept it requires a master architect; in execution, the labors of many.   [262

Pacem in Terris Conference
New York City
February 17, 1965

... Peace will not come through military victory alone. Nor will peace come by good intentions. Peace comes to those who earn it, work for it, sacrifice for it.

Peace will be won only through the untiring practical efforts of this generation and others to follow—efforts to improve the conditions of man's life. It will be won only when all men realize that they share a common destiny on this planet. Peace will be won when starvation, ignorance and injustice are eradicated from a world which has the resources to defeat them.

There is no alternative to peace. Let us pursue it with perseverance and patience.   [263

Arlington Memorial Cemetery
Washington, D. C.
November 11, 1965

... There is an old Hebrew legend that God created many worlds before He finally chose the one in which He placed man. Joining our faith with action, it is today our task to make the world that God gave us a world of peace, of freedom, and of human brotherhood.   [264

National Conference of
Christians and Jews
New York City
June 28, 1966

... There is no quick and easy way to peace—it must and will be built out of the cumulative acts of men and women who dedicate their lives to the service of their fellow men—and therefore to the service of God.   [265

Quote Magazine
March, 1967

... Education for peace, food for peace, health for peace—these are practical and basic ways in which we Americans may help meet mankind's plea for something more than a struggle for everyday existence.   [266

National Association for Secondary
School Principals
February 7, 1966

. . . Choose concern for your fellow man—choose to treat others as you would be treated. Choose to commit yourself to that ultimate political goal: a world "where the strong are just, the weak secure and the peace preserved."   [267

University of California
Berkeley, California
October 5, 1964

. . . **America.**   No nation has done more for peace than ours has since World War II. The U.N., the Marshall Plan, Point Four, the Alliance for Progress, the Peace Corps, the International Monetary Fund and World Bank, Food for Peace, the Nuclear Test Ban Treaty—these have come from initiatives worthy of our position of leadership. These have come from our search for peace.   [268

University of Florida
Gainesville, Florida
October 28, 1966

. . . Men and nations must live together—must strive together, must reason together—to obtain the benefits of civilization.   [269

University of California
Berkeley, California
October 5, 1964

. . . A world in which "nation shall not lift up sword against nation" has never existed. Nor has a world ever existed in which God's blessings were truly and justly shared by his children, and in which the rule of peaceful law prevailed. Yet I am convinced that, unless that kind of world is achieved, there is no long-term hope for the human family—not with the powerful destructive weapons now at man's disposal.   [270

United Jewish Appeal
New York City
December 10, 1966

... The works of peace—as well as the words of peace—are imperative in American foreign policy.   [271

National Conference on
Higher Education
1959

... The building of a better and more peaceful world will never come from any diplomat's ingenious plan. It will come only from the cumulative acts of men who live their lives in respect for their fellow men, and thus, for God.   [272

National Council of Churches
Miami, Florida
December 7, 1966

... We know that peace can be threatened by other forces than armies crossing borders and bombs and missiles falling from the sky. Peace can be threatened by social and economic deprivation, by destitution and hunger. If we are not concerned about "peace-keeping" in all its aspects, then we dare not ignore this explosive threat which can erupt at any time.

And it is time we learn that peace-keeping pertains not only to military forces and United Nations machinery. Peace-keeping pertains to every force that disturbs or threatens to disturb the peace of mankind.　　　　　　[273

Fordham University
Bronx, New York
June 9, 1965

... Peace will have to be built by a hundred thousand individual, positive acts. For peace will not be built by any grand gesture or magical formula. It will be built in the hot streets and muddy fields of countries which did not even exist 20 years ago. It will be built in long months of tireless, patient negotiation over the most minor international issues. It will be built by *people* possessing knowledge of their world and its complexities.　　　　　　　　[274

Tennessee Education Association
Memphis, Tennessee
April 1, 1966

... Peace will not be secured merely by putting out fires, as they occur. We must build a world in which they will be less likely to break out in the first place.　　　　　[275

NATO Parliamentarians
New York City
October 5, 1965

... For as strong and as rich as we may become, our goal of a just and peaceful world will never be achieved by America alone. It will be achieved only when the resources of strong and weak, rich and poor alike are allocated, in the most efficient manner possible, to challenges that are far too great for any one nation or group of nations to attempt to overcome.   [276

Associated Press
New York City
April 25, 1966

... Peace can be found in fertile fields and pastures, in productive peasants and farmers, in workers, in teachers, businessmen, soldiers, and servants of the people who have the vision of a better day and are not afraid to devote their lives to it.   [277

Huron College
Huron, South Dakota
May 31, 1966

... Peace is more than a wish or speech or treaty. Peace is food and fiber. It is health and education.   [278

Huron College
Huron, South Dakota
May 31, 1966

PLATITUDES

. . . Platitudes rarely change attitudes. And baneful criticism and vapid exhortations are cheap substitutes for hard thought and analysis.   [279

Syracuse University
June 6, 1965

POLITICS

. . . Early in my career, I taught political science. For the past twenty years, I have practiced it.   [280

Georgetown University
Washington, D. C.
March 25, 1966

. . . In the highly charged world of American politics, there are great joys and a magnificent sense of work being done, of problems being solved, of accomplishment. If it is hard work, it is good work. It is enterprise in the freest sense, where a man is continually risking his reputation and his record, where his judgment is constantly being tested, where his survival and success depend not only upon his ability but also upon his courage.   [281

"The Cause Is Mankind"
Praeger

... I like contests. I like competition. And I know that some of you will point out that I've chosen the right occupation for it.   [282

> Corn-Picking Contest
> Utica, Nebraska
> October 4, 1966

... Politics is a serious business, not a boy's game where you can pick up the ball and run home if things don't go according to your idea of who should win.   [283

> Press Conference
> 1960

... The vocation of the politician includes the task of dealing with fallen angels—of restraining evil-doers—of mitigating man's inhumanity to man. In positive terms, our task is to create the external conditions for social justice, human dignity and freedom. But we must be willing to accept man as he is—to work with the material at hand. This is surely at the core of our democratic faith and democratic institutions.   [284

> "Christianity and Crisis"
> 25th Anniversary
> New York City
> February 25, 1966

... **Business.** All of us agree there is an intimate relationship between business and politics. In fact, we could easily compare an election to a business investment. Each American has an invaluable asset to invest: his vote.   [285

Luncheon, Business Executives
Los Angeles, California
October 2, 1964

... Democrats-Republicans.   We vote Democratic so we can live like Republicans.   [286

Quote Magazine
April, 1967

... Educator.   A politician must also be an educator, if he is to be effective.   [287

Georgetown University
Washington, D. C.
March 25, 1966

... Purpose.   This is the essence of politics: to translate the concerns and the creative responses of a vast citizenry into effective and humane laws. And, I submit, no country does it better than ours.   [288

Syracuse University
June 6, 1965

POLLUTION (AIR AND WATER)

... Man is the only animal who has succeeded in contaminating virtually every square inch of his surroundings. But what he has done, he is surely capable of undoing. So let us here and now resolve not to rest until we have cleansed our waters, so that we can use them in safety—and cleared the air, so that we can all breathe easier. [289

Gannon College
Erie, Pennsylvania
October 11, 1966

... When we launch astronauts into space, we equip them with special suits, put them in costly capsules, and take every precaution to ensure that they will survive their strange and hostile environment. It seems to me that, here on earth, we have a right to breathe free and easy in the open air—and enjoy life, liberty, and the pursuit of happiness without resorting to smog masks. It is only very recently that our smarting and watery eyes have opened up to the fact that many of us are living at the bottom of another kind of ocean—the atmosphere—which is becoming more and more contaminated and inimical to our health. [290

Gannon College
Erie, Pennsylvania
October 11, 1966

... **The Effluent Society.** We speak of individuals as being spoiled by success. It is our own spectacular economic success, particularly in recent years, which has resulted in the massive spoilage of our air and water. As industry has boomed, as cars and freeways and people have multiplied—so the wear and tear on our natural environment has doubled and re-doubled. Unfortunately, our affluent society has also been an effluent society. [291

Gannon College
Erie, Pennsylvania
October 11, 1966

...Los Angeles. Only a few years ago, smog was regarded as an affliction peculiar to Los Angeles—and a favorite target of comedians' jokes. Now, the laugh is on the rest of us—and, if we're laughing at all, it's often through smog-induced tears. [292

Gannon College
Erie, Pennsylvania
October 11, 1966

POVERTY

...It is hard for us, in the comfort, convenience, and security that most of us enjoy, to truly know what life is like for those on the outside of affluence and well-being. [293

National Association of Secondary
School Principals
Cleveland, Ohio
February 7, 1966

...Contrary to what most people think, less than one-fourth of the families classified as poor receive any public assistance whatever. Most of the poor work—and they work hard. [294

"War on Poverty"
McGraw-Hill

. . . The War on Poverty will be pressed forward until this bitter word "poverty" is banished not only from our lives, but hopefully even from the language we speak. In the dictionaries of the future, it may still appear—but I hope with the designation "Obsolete." [295

*North Carolina Mutual Life Insurance
Company Building Dedication
Durham, North Carolina
April 2, 1966*

. . . We are determined to tear down the tattered tarpaper that separates our growing, prosperous America from the "other America"—the America of one-sixth of our citizens who are citizens only in name. [296

*Americana Hotel
New York, N. Y.
October 31, 1966*

. . . Is there a higher calling than liberating millions of our fellow Americans from the vicious trap of deprivation and defeat? Is there any task more vital than improving the quality of life for every American? [297

*Quote Magazine
May, 1965*

... Just as we are determined to be the first nation to put men on the moon, so we are determined to be the first to put its people—all its people—on their feet here on earth.   [298

> *West Virginia AFL-CIO Legislative*
> *Conference*
> *Charleston, West Virginia*
> *February 8, 1967*

... Human Dignity. The most intangible, but most important, direction in which we need to move is toward the enhancement of human dignity.

That is why community action programs are so important a part of the war on poverty. That is why the participation of the poor in the development and management of these programs is absolutely vital. For the essence of human dignity is the right of people to have a say in determining their own future.

We need to use a new kind of grammar in speaking and writing about poverty—a grammar in which the poor are the subjects, the people who act, rather than the objects, the people who are acted upon. We need to involve the poor actively because we need to learn from them. We need to find out why it is that our schools are not reaching many of their children, why urban renewal is not really eliminating slums, and why welfare programs are not breaking the cycle of dependency. And I think we would do well to listen to people who have hard, first-hand knowledge about all this.

Moreover, we must apply the basic principle of democracy—that people, in their wisdom and even in their folly, know what is best for them. We need to bear in mind

George Bernard Shaw's cautionary words: "Do not do unto others as you would they should do unto you—their tastes may not be the same."   [299

Temple University
Philadelphia, Pennsylvania
June 16, 1966

POWER

. . . We have discovered that the more widely we share our responsibilities, the more we increase our power to meet them.

I sometimes think that many of us got the wrong steer about this in our civics courses. We learned to think of the sum total of power as fixed and unchanging. According to this assumption, whatever powers accrued to one level of government, the others lost.

We tended to assume, likewise, that the endowment of international organizations with new powers and responsibilities inevitably meant that the individual nations gave up theirs.

But now we are learning that power is not fixed and constant—that it grows through undertaking and fulfilling responsibilities. Thus, through the sharing of responsibility, each level of government can gain in strength and capability —as an athlete develops his muscles by exercise.   [300

Brigham Young University
Provo, Utah
October 21, 1966

... The history of our era has taught us that peace is best preserved through strength—strength used with restraint, with wisdom, and with a clear sense of perspective.   [301

> *Minneapolis, Minnesota*
> *October 24, 1964*

PRESIDENCY

... The American Presidency is not a place for a man who is impetuous at one moment, and indecisive the next; nor is it a place for one who is violently for something one day and violently opposed to it on the next, nor is it an office where statements on matters of major policy are so confusing and too contradictory that neither friend nor foe knows where he stands.   [302

> *Acceptance Address*
> *Democratic Convention*
> *August 28, 1964*

... Today the President of the United States is the one and only man in the free world who, by a single error in judgment, a momentary lapse in responsibility, can risk its annihilation.   [303

> *Springfield, Missouri*
> *September 14, 1964*

... The President is the people's lobbyist.   [304

> *Rockefeller Public Service Awards*
> *Washington, D. C.*
> *December 8, 1965*

132

... The constituency of the Presidency is the nation at large, and it is this constituency which the executive branch must bear in mind. And the needs of the nation will not always be reflected in the Washington lobbies, in pressure mail, or in newspaper editorials. Sometimes, it will require great tenacity and curiosity to discover these needs. But this is the job of the men and women who help the President bear the executive burdens.   [305

Rockefeller Public Service Awards
Washington, D. C.
December 8, 1965

... Childlike answers cannot solve man-sized problems. These problems demand leadership that is prudent, restrained, responsible. They require a President who knows that Rome was not built in a day, but who also knows that the great edifice of western civilization can be brought down in ruins in one hour.   [306

Acceptance Address
Democratic Convention
August 28, 1964

PRESIDENCY (PREPARATION FOR)

... Nobody knows what a man would be like if he had the awesome problems of leadership until he is tested. But the people are entitled to know that I have learned the plays and the formations. To the best of my ability, I have tried to prepare for leadership, if need be.   [307

Grit
November 13, 1966

133

PROPAGANDA

... Propaganda, to be effective, must be believed. To be believed, it must be credible. To be credible, it must be true.

[308

Edward R. Murrow Center of
Public Diplomacy
Medford, Massachusetts
December 6, 1965

... The evil genius Joseph Goebbels taught us unfounded propaganda can be effective only if the big lie is so bold and monstrous as to appear uninventable.

[309

Edward R. Murrow Center of
Public Diplomacy
Medford, Massachusetts
December 6, 1965

... We have permitted the Communists very nearly to appropriate the word "peace"—to pose as the peace-makers and to tag us with the label of "war-mongers."

[310

National Conference on
Higher Education
1959

... In real life, unlike in Shakespeare, the sweetness of the rose depends upon the name it bears. Things are not only what they are. They are, in very important respects, what they seem to be. [311

Foreign Service Association
Washington, D. C.
March 26, 1966

PUBLIC OFFICE

... The Long View. I've been told that people who take a long view in public office often take a long rest—at request of the voters. Yet we live in a world in which the impetuous act, the grasp for short-run gain, the sudden loss of judgment could plunge us all into disaster. [312

National Governors Conference
Los Angeles, California
July 6, 1966

... Tenure. Since becoming a United States Senator, and now Vice President, I have welcomed any speaking engagement on a college campus. As a refugee from the classroom—a former professor of political science—I am careful to keep my academic credentials in order. A politician never forgets the precarious nature of elective life. We have never established the practice of tenure in public office.
[313

National Students Association
University of Wisconsin
August 23, 1965

PUBLIC OPINION

... When people generally are aware of a problem, it can be said to have entered the public *consciousness*. When people get up on their hind legs and holler, the problem has not only entered the public consciousness—it has also become a part of the public conscience. At that point, things in our democracy begin to hum. [314

Gannon College
Erie, Pennsylvania
October 11, 1966

... American public opinion is like an ocean—it cannot be stirred by a teaspoon. [315

Gannon College
Erie, Pennsylvania
October 11, 1966

... In my twenty years of public service—as mayor, as Senator, and as Vice-President—I have taken the approach of the educator. For I believe that the way enlightened ideas become public policy is through the enlistment of support and active advocacy by enlightened, informed *people*. [316

National Association of Secondary
School Principals
Cleveland, Ohio
February 7, 1966

... If responsible leaders fail to act affirmatively and constructively, they lose the battle. If they wait for "public opinion to jell," the leadership role inevitably will be seized by racial extremists. Public opinion must be considered in shaping policy, but policy in itself is a powerful determinant of that opinion. [317

> *"Integration vs. Segregation"*
> *Crowell*

PUBLIC SERVICE

... Every government in history has found ways to honor those who render outstanding service. But our own government has never completely solved the problem of how to pay tribute to men and women whose performance in public service has been exceptional. [318

> *Rockefeller Public Service Awards*
> *Washington, D. C.*
> *December 8, 1965*

... The federal service is a dynamic service, an imaginative service, a service whose top executives should be intimately and courageously identified with the program and platform of their President. [319

> *Rockefeller Public Service Awards*
> *Washington, D. C.*
> *December 8, 1965*

... **Bureaucracy.** It is all too easy for the government official to become a bureaucrat. It is all too easy to forget that ours is a government *for* the people and that those in government are in public service, not self-service.   [320

Rockefeller Public Service Awards
Washington, D. C.
December 8, 1965

...Executive Branch. Indeed, it is remarkable that the executive branch of our nation, which has accumulated both power and responsibility over the years, has maintained a tradition of humility and service—and has erected stringent standards of honesty which have reduced corruption to levels far below those, I must say, which exist in many non-public activities.   [321

Rockefeller Public Service Awards
Washington, D. C.
December 8, 1965

...Federal Executives. Time and again I have seen the bright ideas of federal executives, often well below the top echelon, become major national programs. Medicare, for example, is a concept which came to life on the desk of a junior executive some 25 years ago.   [322

Rockefeller Public Service Awards
Washington, D. C.
December 8, 1965

...Federal Executives. I do not believe that any executive or any branch of government like the Executive Branch has a monopoly of wisdom.   [323

Economic Club of Detroit
October 22, 1965

QUACKS (POLITICAL)

... I began my professional career as a pharmacist. I had some opportunity to see quacks at work, and found they came in two brands. The journeyman quack had to find someone who was really ill before he could peddle his nostrum. The really accomplished quack, however, could take a man who was fit as a fiddle, scare him into thinking he was gravely ill, and sell him a useless remedy for a disease he didn't have. [324

Flint, Michigan
September 25, 1964

$\cdot\cdot$ R $\cdot\cdot$

RACISM

. . . We must reject calls for racism, whether they come from a throat that is white or one that is black. I am against racism of any color. [325

NAACP Convention
Los Angeles, California
July 6, 1966

REALISM AND IDEALISM

. . . To be realistic today is to be visionary. To be realistic is to be starry-eyed. [326

White House Conference on
International Cooperation
November 29, 1965

REGULATORY AGENCIES

. . . The regulatory agency which becomes in time, the meek handmaiden of the regulated, is an old story. It is seldom—at the least in our government—a result of the corruption of bribes. It is more often a result of laziness, or lack of interest, which is a more serious danger to good government than venality.   [327

Rockefeller Public Service Awards
Washington, D. C.
December 8, 1965

RELIGIOUS FAITH

... To me, religious faith must be more than an exercise in theology, dogma, ritual or doctrine. It must be a part of one's life. And the Christian faith, to be an effective force in the modern world, must have practical meaning in the lives of those who inhabit the earth.   [328

National Council of Churches
Miami, Florida
December 7, 1966

... My religious conviction is that the way you treat people is the way you treat God.   [329

National Council of Churches
Miami, Florida
December 7, 1966

... **Service.** I believe that each of us has an obligation to serve God at each level of his existence and within each institution of his society—from doing honor to one's parents and children to performing his work with dignity and honesty to playing his role within his school, his neighborhood, his church, his community and nation. [330

National Council of Churches
Miami, Florida
December 7, 1966

... Service. Suppose a brother or sister is in rags with not enough food for the day, and one of you says, "Good luck to you, keep yourselves warm and have plenty to eat," but does nothing to supply their bodily needs, what is the good of that? So with faith; if it does not lead to action it is in itself a lifeless thing. [331

National Conference of
Christians and Jews
New York City
June 28, 1966

REPUBLICAN PARTY

... Those who have kidnapped the Republican Party have made it this year not a party of memory and sentiment, but one of stridency, of unrestrained passion, of extreme and radical language. [332

Acceptance Address
Democratic National Convention
August 28, 1964

... Tonight is a Republican holiday: tonight is Halloween. All across our country the Republican faithful are hud-

dled together to hear the Barry Goldwaters and the Richard
Nixons conjure up all the gremlins, all the demons, all the
scare stories they use to frighten good citizens under their
beds. [333

Americana Hotel
New York, N.Y.
October 31, 1966

REVOLUTION

... Every day we see peoples caught between soaring
hopes and immovable traditions. Each day we learn anew
that the disorder which persists cannot be ended by political
maneuver or military power alone. We learn anew of outbreaks of violence and turbulence, or peaceful revolutions
turned into violent ones. We learn anew of disorder which
invites Communism—which so often comes as the scavenger
of ruined revolutions. [334

Catholic Education Center
Chicago, Illinois
January 31, 1966

... The revolutionary process is turbulent and fraught
with dangers. It contains the danger of unbridled competing
nationalisms; the lure of false prophets and demogogues; the
temptation of illusory short-cuts that lead to new tyranny;
the passions aroused by unfulfilled expectations. [335

West Point, New York
June 8, 1966

144

... History teaches us that the great revolutions aren't started by people who are utterly down and out, without hope and vision. They take place when people begin to live a little better—and when they see how much yet remains to be achieved.   [336

> North Carolina Mutual Life Insurance
>   Company Building Dedication
> Durham, North Carolina
> April 2, 1966

ROOSEVELT, FRANKLIN D.

... I grew up in an America in which the federal government did very little to fulfill one of the major purposes for which it was created and here I quote directly from the preamble of our Constitution—to "promote the general welfare." This was the battle which Franklin Delano Roosevelt and his New Deal liberals fought and won—to get the federal government to assume and fulfill its share of responsibility for the general welfare of the American people. [337

> International Newspaper
>   Advertising Executives
> Washington, D. C.
> January 26, 1967

· · S · ·

SCHOLARS (IN GOVERNMENT)

... Today, Washington is brimming with visiting advisers, witnesses, consultants, and technical experts from our universities in every field of human knowledge. Washington National Airport, at any point in time during the day, includes, in transit, a faculty which—if kept together—would create one of the world's most distinguished institutions of higher education. These professors are valuable to Washington precisely because they are unfettered, and because they often have an opportunity to see beyond the immediate urgencies and rigidities of ongoing operations. [338

Rutgers University
New Brunswick, New Jersey
September 22, 1966

SCHOOLS (INTEGRATION)

... The problem in the North and West is less one of establishing desegregation than it is that of achieving meaningful integration. For many years to come, the task of preventing the continuation and growth of schools composed almost entirely of Negro, Puerto Rican, or Mexican students will test the good will and judgment of all concerned. Our public schools, of course, will bear the major responsibility for providing special educational programs and opportunities for the culturally deprived minorities. In preventing integration from being circumvented by residential segregation, the schools again must play an important role. But they cannot carry the total burden of responsibility for solving the problems of denied equal rights throughout our society.   [339

"Integration vs. Segregation"
Crowell

... Our society cannot refuse the Negro an equal education and then refuse to employ him in a decent job on the grounds that he is untrained. We cannot follow a deliberate policy of apartheid and then say we refuse to have our children associate with the Negro because of differences in behavior. Such differences as exist result from this very pattern of forcing the Negro's exclusion from the mainstream of American life.   [340

"Integration vs. Segregation"
Crowell

... The Constitution is color-blind; it should no more be violated to attempt integration than to preserve segregation. This does not mean that a community can be blind to the racial composition of its schools, or that it should fail to strive for the best educational environment: one that in cutting across economic, cultural, and racial lines exposes the student to a microcosm of our society.   [341

"Integration vs. Segregation"
Crowell

SCIENCE AND TECHNOLOGY

... The world of science is the world of man's greatest adventure. It is an adventure far beyond that begun by Columbus or by Alexander the Great or by Cortez. It is an adventure into the unknown. It is the search into the deep secrets which may yield answers far beyond man's hope. It is the place for the man or woman who will devote himself, through long hours of labor and difficulty, to mankind's cause. It is the place where years of dedication and effort may yield little. Yet it is the place where discovery and accomplishment can bring a sense of reward and exhilaration that comes to few people.   [342

> *National Youth Science Camp*
> *Washington, D. C.*
> *July 13, 1966*

... We must deliberately direct the miraculous achievements of science and technology to the fulfillment of human needs. Only thus will man prove himself worthy of the incalculable powers for good and evil which science has placed in his hands. Science can destroy us—but it can also save us. The awesome force of atomic energy can mean catastrophe—or it can be a mighty force for peace and well-being. There is nothing inherently threatening in man's spirit— and the depth of his commitment to peace on earth. [343

> *University of Minnesota at Duluth*
> *June 10, 1966*

... I believe that our almost breathtaking scientific and technological revolutions have provided man with a new opportunity to build a truly human world. I believe that the growing interdependence of mankind, caused by these revolutions, can lead to a world community in which both persons and nations find their individuality enhanced and their mutual fate a condition to be welcomed rather than a threat to be feared.   [344

Institute for International Education
December 6, 1966

... All of us—in developed and developing countries, alike, and on both sides of the Iron Curtain—share the desire to make science and technology the servants rather than the master of mankind and its future.   [345

Georgetown University
Washington, D. C.
March 19, 1966

... **Science Gap.** Why are a few nations of the world, mostly in the West, affluent? And why are the many poor? The Marxists had a pat answer. They blamed it on Imperialism. Yet today we see the nations of Europe, divested of their empires, more prosperous than ever before. Actually, it is the science gap that yawns between the two worlds.   [346

Weizmann Institute Dinner
New York
December 6, 1965

... **Technology.** I have noticed that while a breakthrough in science flashes quickly around the world, a breakthrough in technology may take years to find its way to a place of need. What we should seek, therefore, are rules and practices to help speed the flow of technology, not slow it down or stop it. [347

Department of Commerce Symposium
on Technology and World Trade
Washington, D. C.
November 16, 1966

... **Technology.** You do not have to reconcile conflicting ideologies to agree on international safety standards for aerial navigation, on the international allocation and use of radio frequencies, and on a global weather reporting system. The technological imperatives of the modern world have long since transcended national frontiers. [348

White House Conference
on International Cooperation
November 29, 1965

SEA

... Our dreams for the oceans are not those of poets and prophets but those of practical men, convinced by our oceanic tradition that we can develop the bountiful resources of the seas—as we have those on land—to solve man's pressing needs for food, water, minerals and energy. [349

Seattle Area Industrial Council
September 28, 1966

SLUMS

... The promise of freedom is like rays of the rising sun dispelling the shadows of night. Today these rays are reaching into the darkest corners of our urban ghettoes and rural slums. But we must now persevere until the sun has risen completely—until the hopelessness and despair of the long night of bondage is transformed into a shining day of freedom and opportunity.

The urban ghetto is little more than a highly complex ingrained and self-sustaining system which ruthlessly and systematically denies to residents of these areas any opportunity for meaningful choice in housing, education, jobs, welfare and public services. And it is this inability to choose—this denial of the right to chart one's destiny and to be a real participant in the social, economic and political life of this country—which produces the frustration, bitterness, hopelessness and outrage we encounter today in the urban ghettoes of America.   [350

> *National Fellowship Award Dinner*
> *Philadelphia, Pennsylvania*
> *May 23, 1966*

... Despite the recent efforts to improve the lives of those persons consigned to live in the slums and ghettoes of our cities, we must recognize that little has changed in their daily lives. We still find the poorest schools there—not the best. In those areas where young people are usually denied broad exposure to culture, the arts and society generally, we find schools that often do little to compensate for it. It is

152

time to see that educational excellence exists everywhere—but especially in those areas where it is needed most urgently. [351

*American Personnel and
Guidance Association
Washington, D. C.
April 4, 1966*

... Slumism is poverty, illiteracy, disease. Slumism is discrimination and frustration and bitterness. Slumism is ungathered garbage and dilapidated buildings. Slumism is a family of eight in an unheated room. Slumism is danger on the stair and violence in the street. Slumism is rent so high a desperate man is moved to tears or crime. Slumism is the pent-up anger of people living on the outside of affluence. Slumism is decay of structure and deterioration of the human spirit. Slumism is a virus which spreads through the body politic. As other "isms," it breeds disorder and demogoguery and hate. [352

*U. S. Conference of Mayors
Dallas, Texas
June 13, 1966*

... It is one thing to cry "Freedom Now" on a picket line. But it is another to achieve true freedom in the squalid world of the ghetto—where generations of exploitation have produced problems which no man can overcome in a day, a week or a year—where we see and feel the devastating impact of the tragic equation which has too often decreed that poor shall beget poor, that ignorance shall beget misery.

[353

National Catholic Social Action Conference
Georgetown University
Washington, D. C.
August 26, 1966

... People without hope—people caught by the vicious forces of the ghetto—are easy prey for those who seek to destroy and disrupt our efforts to build a more just and free society.

[354

Conference with City Managers
Washington, D. C.
July 28, 1966

... We know our problems. We talk about them, in the abstract, as slums, crime, crowding, lack of clean air, over-burdened schools, inadequate transportation, a shortage of playgrounds and parks, and the need for revenue. But they are, to the human beings living in the ghettoes of our great cities, far more immediate. They are problems of people—of old people living on miserably small incomes, in single, musty, lonely rooms, of children whose play areas are littered uncleaned gutters. Negro families denied housing everywhere but in the ghetto, paying exorbitant rent for un-

heated apartments, poor men and women falling victim after
dark to robbery and violence. [355

Urban America Conference
Washington, D. C.
September 13, 1966

... We have learned that no prosperous American neighborhood can really be secure amid other neighborhoods filled
with poverty and pent-up anger. We have learned that no
business can operate at maximum efficiency until those who
are unemployed find work, that no city can provide the best
in life until the worst of its slums come open to the light, and
that our children cannot achieve the fullness of the future
until the children of others can share in it. [356

United States Junior
Chamber of Commerce
Detroit, Michigan
June 29, 1966

... **Violence.** We cannot condone or excuse violence—
whatever the cause—nor can we overlook the role of
hoodlums and agitators in certain of the disorders. We
cannot condone rioting and civil disorder. But we can—and
we must—learn from these outbreaks that a major factor in
our remaining problems of human rights is the vicious and

interlocking system of the ghetto which mercilessly strips all vestiges of humanity from its victims. [357

National Catholic Social
Action Conference
Georgetown University
Washington, D. C.
August 26, 1966

. . . In the terrible rioting and violence which has gripped our cities, we can often discover twisted and mistaken attempts to achieve a sense of self-respect and self-sacrifice by persons who blindly retaliate against a society that has seemingly denied them all chance to achieve their humanity in acceptable ways. [358

National Catholic Social
Action Conference
Georgetown University
Washington, D. C.
August 26, 1966

THE SOUTH

. . . In the past and present, the South has given to America, and to the world, men and women of leadership. We must see to it that *all* the people of the South have a chance to obtain education that will allow them to develop their potentials for leadership. [359

Southern Conference on Education
Richmond, Virginia
December 2, 1965

... There is a new South as well as an old South, and it is rapidly gaining ground. The leaders of this new South recognize that Negro and white people have far more to gain from cooperation than from conflict.   [360

*North Carolina Mutual Life Insurance
Company Building Dedication
Durham, North Carolina
April 2, 1966*

... We are challenged to lift the yoke of poverty from one-fifth of our fellow citizens, to reverse the tragic equation which has too often decreed that poor shall beget poor and ignorance shall beget misery. Nowhere is that equation more accurate, or its consequences more devastating, than in our own American Southland, where almost one-half the families live below the poverty line. What a burden this is on the South—in terms of welfare costs, of lost productivity, of stress on your society.   [361

*First Annual Public Affairs Conference
Atlanta, Georgia
November 19, 1965*

SPACE AGE

... **Discovery.** We live in times today even more challenging than "The Age of Discoveries" centuries ago, when the world was opening to the daring seafarers of Spain and England. I can recall reading of those voyages—made in tiny ships only a little less cramped than our spacecraft—when I was a boy. And I remember my keen regret that everything had been discovered, that never again would men set foot for the first time on a new land.   [362

San Fernando Valley State College
California
September 26, 1966

... It used to be said that the sky was the only limit to human aspiration and achievement. Now—thanks to man's ingenuity and spirit of adventure—we are bursting through into the infinity of space. And as we look toward that infinity, we are inevitably reminded of St. Augustine's words: "Man looks about the universe in awe at its wonders—and forgets that he himself is the greatest wonder of all."   [363

San Fernando Valley State College
California
September 26, 1966

... Space activities—even competition in space—can be a substitute for aggression, a bridge for mutual understanding and the identification of common interests with other nations, and a major tool of arms control and disarmament.
                                                        [364

San Fernando Valley State College
California
September 26, 1966

... Ever since Copernicus, we have realized that our earth is a mere speck in an immense universe. But while we have known this intellectually and theoretically, most of us have not really taken it to heart, not really felt it in the marrow of our bones. As the full significance of that fact is brought home to us by the actual exploration of space—as we begin to comprehend that the earth itself is a kind of manned spaceship hurtling through the infinity of space—it will seem increasingly absurd that we have not better organized the life of the human family.   [365

San Fernando Valley State College
California
September 26, 1966

. . . Fifty years ago Carl Sandburg wrote these lines describing the limit of man's technological achievement up to that time: "I am riding on a limited express, one of the crack trains of the nation. Hurtling across the prairie into blue haze and dark air go fifteen all-steel coaches holding a thousand people . . . I ask a man in the smoker where he is going and he answers: " 'Omaha.' " Carl Sandburg still writes his poetry, but the "smoker" is in outer space.   [366

Institute for International Education
New York City
December 6, 1966

SPHERE OF INFLUENCE

. . . If today there is a proper American "sphere of influence" it is this fragile sphere called earth upon which all men live and share a common fate—a sphere where our influence must be for peace and justice. [367

Buffalo Club
Buffalo, New York
January 6, 1967

STEVENSON, ADLAI

... Adlai Stevenson sought to maximize the element of rationality in politics. As an experienced political leader, he knew that one of the difficulties of being reasonable in an irrational world is that you have a small clientele. No public man in our time did more to enlarge the clientele of reason in politics. [368

Catholic Education Center
Chicago, Illinois
January 31, 1966

·· T ··

TALENT

... How many millions of talents today lie unused, or woefully underused, because: There was no money. There was no encouragement. There was no hope, back at the crossroads of life. [369

National PTA Convention
Baltimore, Maryland
May 17, 1966

... One day recently I visited an old couple living in a southwestern city. I noticed a piano in the corner of their old-fashioned living room. "Does anyone ever play on that piano?" I asked. The old man replied: "No, no one plays on it now, but there is a heap of fine music in there if you could just get it out." I am reminded of that piano and that old man's words as I think of the young people in Washington and other American communities. There is a heap of fine talent in these young people—if we can only get it out. [370

Urban League Back-To-School Rally
Washington, D. C.
August 25, 1966

TARIFFS AND TRADE

... There was a time when tariffs produced revenue and protected young and infant industries. But the rich Western world of which we are a part has long since learned, I hope, that the barriers to trade—both tariff and other barriers—often become excuses to protect uncompetitive domestic industries. [371

Economic Club of Detroit
October 22, 1965

... Trade routes are vital arteries of international cooperation. They can be among the most significant of the bridges of better understanding between the Free World, the Soviet Union, and the Eastern European countries. Expansion of trade between such diverse economic systems needs the development of special ground rules consistant with Free World trade practices. [372

American Agricultural Editors'
Association
Washington, D. C.
June 22, 1966

TAX-SHARING

... Washington abounds today with proposals for federal revenue-sharing with states and localities. Let me say first that we already share substantial amounts of federal revenue with our state and local governments.

You might be surprised to know that state and local governments will derive about 17 per cent of their total revenue from the federal government during the coming year.

This is not to reject proposals for further revenue-sharing. But I think we must take a long and careful look at them.

I do not think, for example, that the federal government would be keeping proper faith with American taxpayers if tax revenues were to be handed over, no strings attached—as some have proposed—to state and local governments which might not be ready or able to use them effectively.

Methods of distribution would have to be devised, and, above all, problems of allocation among the states and among the various levels of government would have to be solved.

Tax-sharing is not a panacea. It should not be oversimplified, as a few people have attempted to do. However, it *is* worth serious consideration and thorough debate—and I expect that to be forthcoming in the year ahead. [373

International Newspaper
Advertising Executives
Washington, D. C.
January 26, 1967

TEACHERS

... President Johnson began his career as a teacher and so did I. There is no question in his mind—nor in mine—that education is at the heart of national, social, economic and political development. [374

Georgetown University
Washington, D. C.
March 19, 1966

... Already, the teacher is as important in our international relations as the diplomat or the soldiers. Tomorrow may he be even more important. [375

DeKalb County Education Association
Atlanta, Georgia
April 29, 1966

THIRD WORLD (DEVELOPING NATIONS)

... There are, in this world, conditions which not only bring a sense of shame and insufficiency to those of us who live in such a blessed land, but which can lead to the eruption of the little disorder, which can grow to the small war, which can build to the cataclysm which could destroy rich and poor, black and white, believer and non-believer—all of us alike. [376

Michigan State University
East Lansing, Michigan
June 12, 1966

...Tonight, as I address this audience, most of mankind goes to bed hungry. Many millions can neither read nor write. Many millions are physically ill. Yet these people have learned how to fight and die for what they believe in. That's the kind of world that we face. [377

Economic Club of Detroit
October 22, 1965

. . . This world cannot rest upon a base of hungry, needy, ignorant, and despairing people without sooner or later experiencing a violent explosion. [378

*Huron College
Huron, South Dakota
May 31, 1966*

. . . People in places many of us never heard of, whose names we can't pronounce or even spell, are speaking up for themselves. They speak in languages we once classified as "exotic" but whose mastery is now essential for our diplomats and businessmen. But what they say is very much the same the world over. They want a decent standard of living. They want human dignity and a voice in their own futures. They want their children to grow up strong and healthy and free.
[379

*Shattuck School
Faribault, Minnesota
June 4, 1966*

. . . There is a growing recognition that the gap between the affluent and the poor nations is the primordial problem of our times. It is at once massive, stubborn and urgent. It is understandable in simple terms of human morality. But it can be solved only by the most imaginative and far-reaching measures, involving all of our countries in a cooperative effort that must be sustained for years. [380

*Organization for Economic Cooperation
    and Development
Paris, France
April 7, 1967*

. . . East-West. While the emergent peoples of the world *are* vitally interested in the great East-West struggle, they are primarily engrossed in their own struggle to find a way up—at almost any cost—from the mire of famine and disease, from the filth and rags of "native quarters," from degrading ignorance, from the outcast, almost subhuman status assigned to them by a civilization which stumbled into the industrial revolution two or three centuries before they did.   [381

National Conference on
Higher Education
1959

. . . Education. Education is a powerful personal ideal to people in the underdeveloped countries. It is also indispensable to their economic progress and national independence. At one time, it was the rather simple belief that the reason some countries were poor and laggard was simply that they lacked the necessary capital and know-how. But we are coming to understand that money and techniques are not enough.   [382

National Conference on
Higher Education
1959

. . . Nation Building. Quite properly we emphasize the "ics"—physics, optics, nucleonics. I believe we must emphasize too the "tions"—education, transportation, nutrition, communication, irrigation—the things needed in developing countries—so that both our own citizens and those of developing nations can acquire the useful skills of nation-building. [383

Department of Commerce Symposium
   of Technology and World Trade
Washington, D. C.
November 16, 1966

TOTALITARIANISM

... The difference between the totalitarian and the free man is the difference in outlook about man's relationship to himself and his state and his God. The totalitarian believes that the individual must serve the state. The free man believes that political, economic and social institutions are designed to serve man. [384

Lutheran Youth Conference
Miami Beach, Florida
August 27, 1965

... Fascism and communism have their points of difference, of course. But both are characterized by the rule of a self-chosen, self-perpetuating elite. And it is this elite which arrogates to itself the right not only to govern the people, but to tell them what they may do, where they may go, what they may read, and even how they should think. [385

Order of Ahepa Convention
Washington, D. C.
August 17, 1966

... The forces of totalitarianism do not plan to blow the world to pieces. They plan to pick it up piece by piece as we progressively tire and withdraw. [386

Duke University
Durham, North Carolina
April 24, 1965

TRUMAN, HARRY S.

... Harry Truman "gave 'em hell"—but he never hit below the belt. It would have been totally out of character—and he didn't need to, anyway. [387

Springfield, Missouri
September 14, 1964

... You ended World War II and brought peace to a weary and shattered world. You transformed President Franklin Roosevelt's vision of a United Nations into reality. You took the historic decision to aid Greece and Turkey when the flames of freedom had almost flickered out in that part of the world. You launched and saw through to sensational success the Marshall Plan of aid to the war-torn nations of Europe. In the best American tradition, you aided friend and former foe alike. Mr. President, you were a great builder in your years of high responsibility—a builder of peace, of a new Europe, of Israel-American friendship, and of many other things. [388

Truman Award Banquet
Kansas City, Missouri
December 19, 1965

·· U ··

UNITED NATIONS

... Today we hear voices advocating the abandonment of the United Nations, withdrawal from the United Nations. They are misguided. They would abandon an imperfect instrument for preserving world peace because they dislike our imperfect world. To abandon the United Nations—or to immobilize it through crippling restrictions or failure to support it—would only prove that our generation had forgotten the lessons of half a century of nationalism and isolationism. Let those who would destroy the United Nations recall the international anarchy that followed the demise of the League of Nations. In a nuclear era when anarchy can lead to annihilation, the United Nations deserves the support of all nations—large and small, rich and poor. The heroes of the world community are not those who withdraw when difficulties ensue, not those who can envision neither the prospect of success nor the consequence of failure—but those who stand the heat of battle, the fight for world peace through the United Nations.   [389

Pacem in Terris Conference
New York City
February 17, 1965

169

... The United Nations has survived twenty tumultuous years—and that in itself is a saving miracle. But it has done much more than survive—it has grown in prestige and in power for good. [390

White House Conference
on International Cooperation
November 29, 1965

... The UN is the most articulate expression of modern man's desire for international cooperation and of his recognition of interdependence—cooperation without domination, interdependence without dependence. [391

White House Conference
on International Cooperation
November 29, 1965

... When, through the United Nations, we can achieve something so important as a treaty banning nuclear weapons from outer space, all the months and years of effort are more than repaid. There are those who complain of the loss of sovereignty involved in membership in the United Nations, or in the Organization of American States, or in NATO, or in signing any international treaty. But without the rule of law, the rule of the jungle prevails. And "sovereignty" is lost in the fire and dust of brute power and force. [392

Buffalo Club
Buffalo, New York
January 6, 1967

... Investment. One of the best investments we can make is investment in United Nations peacekeeping—an investment which will save American lives. [393

University of California
Berkeley, California
October 5, 1964

... World Law. The United Nations has proven its value as an institution for world peace. Our faith in it is strong—and our hope is firm that it will one day become what it was intended to be—a world society of nations under law, not merely law backed by force, but law backed by justice and by popular consent. The answer to world war can only be world law. [394

University of California
Berkeley, California
October 5, 1964

·· V ··

VICE PRESIDENCY

... I weighed this decision about the Vice Presidency very carefully—not long, but carefully. If there's one quality I do not have, it's reluctance.   [395

Quote Magazine
February, 1965

... I try harder. I have to. I am only Number Two.   [396

National Association of
Broadcasters
1965

... There is a hazard course every Vice President has to run. It is part of the basic training one has to go through. No man in public life is as much exposed to guerilla war as a Vice President—the opportunity to be shot at from all sides. If you survive, it is a modern-day miracle.   [397

Press Conference
1966

... The President has only 190 million bosses. The Vice President has 190 million and one.   [398

American Salesman Magazine
1966

... President Johnson will see to it that the Vice President earns his pay. President Johnson believes in a day's work for a day's pay, and he'll see to it that anybody around him is an activist, because he is an activist himself.   [399

Quote Magazine
November, 1964

VIETNAM

... The birth of a nation seldom comes without pain and suffering. The South Vietnamese, bled white by the calculated assassination of many of their able leaders, are fumbling their way toward a democratic order. In this there is confusion and tumult. But from our standpoint as liberals: Is the tumult not infinitely preferable to the monolithic silence in Hanoi?   [400

National Convention
Americans for Democratic Action
Washington, D. C.
April 23, 1966

... **Peasants.** The peasants of Vietnam—and, indeed, of all Asia—are rebelling against the kind of life they have led for ages. They want security. But they also want dignity and self-respect, justice and hope of something better in the future. [401

*Columbia Scholastic Press
Association
New York
March 12, 1966*

...Refugees. Some 800,000 refugees have fled to government-controlled areas in South Vietnam during the past year and a half. Like Berliners, they voted with their feet. [402

*National Convention
Americans for Democratic Action
Washington, D. C.
April 23, 1966*

...United States Presence. We are not in Vietnam to build an empire, to exercise domination over that part of the world, or to establish military bases. We are *not* there to impose a government or a way of life on other peoples. [403

*Columbia Scholastic Press
Association
New York
March 12, 1966*

·· W ··

WOMEN

... Despite the fact that we are doing better in this respect than most other countries, it still remains true that the richest under-realized resource in America is the talent of its women.   [404

Holton Arms School
Bethesda, Maryland
May 11, 1966

WORLD LEADERSHIP

... Leadership in today's world requires far more than a large stock of gunboats and a hard fist at the conference table. Leadership today requires more than the ability to go it alone—although we must not be afraid to do so when necessary. Leadership today requires understanding of the problems we face, of the resources at hand, and of the objectives we seek.   [405

University of Florida
Gainesville, Florida
October 28, 1966

... Leadership today requires the ability to lead and inspire others—to lead and inspire in a sense of common enterprise. For strong and rich as we may become, our goal of a just and peaceful world will never be achieved by America alone. It will be achieved only when the resources of strong and weak, of rich and poor alike are allocated, in the most effective manner possible, to challenges that are far too great for any one nation to attempt to overcome. This, then, is the test we must set ourselves: Not to march alone, but to march in such a way that others will wish to join us.

[406

Buffalo Club
Buffalo, New York
January 6, 1967

... We have already eaten breakfast to the accompaniment in our morning newspapers, of too many "Yankee Go Home" signs, too many riots, too many denunciations of ourselves to believe that leadership, even in the cause of peace, can reward us with international laurel wreaths. [407

Huron College
Huron, South Dakota
May 31, 1966

... The mantle of leadership is not a cloak of comfort, but rather the robe of responsibility. Leadership does not permit

178

a person or a nation license or luxury. Leadership imposes responsibility and affords few privileges. [408

American University
Washington, D. C.
June 13, 1965

... It is the prosperous who can most afford compassion and humility. It is the powerful who can most afford patience and perspective. Let us, then, not pursue policies—or judge ourselves—in consonance with the passion of the moment. Let us pursue those courses of which, in the judgment of history, it can be said: "These were the paths taken by wise men." [409

West Point, New York
June 8, 1966

... We hear many voices these days saying that America is over-extended in the world, that other people's problems need not be our problems, that we ought to close up shop overseas and enjoy the affluence here in the good old U. S. A. When that time comes, this nation is doomed. Who in the world will work for democracy if we do not? Who in the world can preserve the peace if we do not? Who in the world can set the example, can offer the needed hand, if we do not? [410

Al Smith Dinner
New York City
October 12, 1965

... I, for one, am determined that the hopes of mankind shall not be in vain—that their faith in the strength and goodness of America shall not be misplaced.   [411

American Personnel and
Guidance Association
Washington, D. C.
April 4, 1966

... World order and the rule of law will be secure on this earth only when men have to cope with the continuing conflicts of peoples and nations through the peaceful processes of bargaining and negotiation. And I might admonish my fellow Americans that we too need to be cognizant of the differences in other lands, that we seek above all to negotiate, to accomodate, to adjust so that peoples realize their hopes in their way.   [412

Syracuse University
June 6, 1965

... I think the strong nation is the one that can speak softly, walk softly, admit her own weaknesses, recognize her own inadequacies—and we've been able to do that.   [413

Economic Club of Detroit
October 22, 1965

... We must be firm without being belligerent. We must be resolute without being arrogant. We must be humble without being weak. We must be strong without being domineering.   [414

Al Smith Dinner
New York
October 13, 1965

... Today we face three great and interrelated tasks in the world: the pursuit of peace; the effort to narrow the gap between the rich and poor nations; and the necessity of sustaining an American economy able to carry a thousand future burdens here and around the world.   [415

Associated Press
New York
April 25, 1966

... The primary responsibility for preserving the independence and security of a country remains with the people and the government of that country. If the people and their leaders have no will to preserve their independence, no outside force can save them. If the government can provide the people with a cause for which to fight, with a program inspiring sacrifice and effort, that government can be capable of defending itself against Communist infiltration and subversion from within. Where subversion from within is supported from outside, as is the case in Vietnam, outside assistance is needed if such a government is to achieve this capability. In many areas of the world, the United States has inherited the role of protector and defender of non-Communist nations which are under Communist assault. It is a role we have not sought. It is often a painful and expensive one. But it is an essential one—both to the security of the non-Communist world and to our own. [416

Michigan State University
Lansing, Michigan
June 1, 1965

WORLD WAR II (ORIGIN)

... Today we know that World War II began not in 1939 or 1941 but in the 1920's and 1930's when those who should have known better persuaded themselves that they were not their brother's keeper. [417

Arlington Memorial Cemetery
November 11, 1965

·· Y ··

YOUTH

... Whenever I meet with young Americans, there is a strong temptation to glorify youth, to attempt to shed the thirty-odd years that separate us, and to tell you that your vitality and enthusiasm are the ultimate virtues.   [418

National Student Association
University of Wisconsin
August 23, 1965

... A mathematician told me recently that, in his field, if a man or woman did not contribute some significant result before age 30—it was too late. While I think he may have been exaggerating for effect—he assured me he was not. He was an old fogey of 33.   [419

National Youth Science Camp
Washington, D. C.
July 13, 1966

...**Action.** We live in a time of ferment, change, anguish, and, ultimately, hope reborn. There is restlessness and questioning—as there should be. The youth of America want to be where the action is—for this is not a beat or silent generation, but one alive with activity, idealism, and compassion.   [420

National Student Association
University of Wisconsin
August 23, 1965

... **Activities.**   Ten years ago our campus bulletin boards were monopolized by notices of social events. Today these same bulletin boards are filled with notices of political activity, of volunteer work, of opportunities to exchange ideas and to be of public service—all outside the classroom itself. [421

University of West Virginia
Morgantown, West Virginia
October 7, 1966

... The next few years of human history will be dangerous ones. But they will also be years of opportunity. For never has mankind possessed such power for good and for making the world safer and happier for hundreds of millions of people who have never had their share of anything but hunger, ignorance and misery. Your generation will have a large part to play in determining whether man destroys himself or whether he moves forward into a new age of

184

peace and understanding. The future is in your hands. I hope you will make the most of it.   [422

Columbia Scholastic Press
Association
New York City
March 12, 1966

... Welcome Aboard.   Progress has ridden no fast express. It has been a local all the way. Thus, as older generations welcome you aboard, I think you ought to know that they've not been cooling their heels waiting for youth.   [423

Michigan State University
East Lansing, Michigan
June 12, 1966

Biography

HUBERT HORATIO HUMPHREY
The Vice President

Hubert Horatio Humphrey, Democrat, of Waverly, Minnesota, was born in Wallace, South Dakota, on May 27, 1911. He is the son of Hubert Horatio Humphrey, Sr. and Christine Sannes Humphrey. On September 3, 1936, he married Muriel Buck of Huron, South Dakota. They have three sons—Hubert Horatio Humphrey, III born June 26, 1942; Robert Andrew Humphrey, born March 26, 1944; Douglas Sannes Humphrey, born February 3, 1948— and one daughter, Nancy (Mrs. C. Bruce Solomonson of Burnsville, Minnesota) born February 27, 1939; three grandchildren, Victoria Solomonson, born November 8, 1960, Jill Solomonson, born March 1, 1962, and Amy Fay Solomonson, born April 9, 1965.

Mr. Humphrey received a degree from the Denver College of Pharmacy in 1933. He received his B.A. degree from the University of Minnesota in 1939. He received his M.A. from Louisiana State University in 1940.

He was elected Mayor of Minneapolis in 1945 and re-elected in 1947. He was elected to the United States Senate in 1948 and re-elected in 1954 and 1960. He was elected Senate Majority Whip in 1961. In 1964 he was elected Vice President for the term beginning January 20, 1965.

He is Chairman of the President's Council on Equal Opportunity, Chairman of the President's Committee on Equal Employment Opportunity, Chairman of the National Aeronautics and Space Council, Chairman of the Peace Corps Advisory Council, Honorary Chairman of the National Advisory Council to the Office of Economic Opportunity, Chairman of the Special Cabinet Task Force on Travel USA, member of the National Security Council, and member of the Board of Regents of the Smithsonian Institution.

INDEX

Index

192

196

About the Editor

Perry D. Hall is a Senior Book Editor of Droke House, Publishers. A former newspaperman, he attended the University of South Carolina and is an Air Force Veteran. He resides in Anderson, S. C. with his wife and two daughters.

Quote

THE QUOTABLE HUBERT HUMPHREY is one of six books of the quotations of the foremost living American political leaders published by Droke House. The series includes THE QUOTABLE HARRY S. TRUMAN, DWIGHT D. EISENHOWER, HUBERT H. HUMPHREY, RICHARD M. NIXON, LYNDON B. JOHNSON and ROBERT F. KENNEDY.

Each book contains quotations showing where these political leaders stand on every important issue of today—as well as where they have stood on important issues of the past: with quotations alphabetized under subject headings for quick reference, with complete index, and biography.

For 27 years, QUOTE, the Weekly Digest for public speakers, has recorded the history of our times in the quotations of the men and women making that history. Working with outstanding editors, the staff of QUOTE has compiled and edited this six volume set of QUOTABLE American Political Leaders.